Towns and Cities

Competing for survival

Angus McIntosh

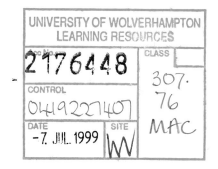

E & FN SPON
An Imprint of Chapman & Hall

London · Weinheim · New York · Tokyo · Melbourne · Madras

**Published by E & FN Spon, an imprint of
Chapman & Hall, 2–6 Boundary Row, London SE1 8HN, UK**

Chapman & Hall, 2–6 Boundary Row, London SE1 8HN, UK

Chapman & Hall, GmbH, Pappelallee 3, 69469 Weinheim, Germany

Chapman & Hall USA, 115 Fifth Avenue, New York, NY 10003, USA

Chapman & Hall Japan, ITP-Japan, Kyowa Building, 3F, 2-2-1 Hirakawacho, Chiyoda-ku, Tokyo 102, Japan

Chapman & Hall Australia, 102 Dodds Street, South Melbourne, Victoria 3205, Australia

Chapman & Hall India, R. Seshadri, 32 Second Main Road, CIT East, Madras 600 035, India

First edition 1997

© 1997 Angus McIntosh

Typeset in 10/12pt Times by Photoprint, Torquay, Devon
Printed in Great Britain by the Alden Press, Osney Mead, Oxford

ISBN 0 419 22740 7

Towns and Cities

To my mother and father

*who encouraged me at an early age
to question the world we live in*

*and to Patricia, Jonathan and Rebecca
who continually surprise and delight me.*

Contents

Acknowledgements

Anyone who is foolish enough to start writing a book knows that the early good intentions are soon reduced to the agony of creating something readable. Combining the writing of a book, in a matter of months, with a full-time job inevitably results in a less than perfect script. My hope is that, despite the inaccuracies, a few of my central messages make sense. If they do, there is no doubt that my conversations over recent months with a number of colleagues, including Keith Wood and Chris Simmons at Richard Ellis and Mark Shepherd at the University of Salford, have helped me clarify my thoughts.

However, without the typing tenacity and help from my secretary Terri-Jean Simmonds the text would never have been completed. My thanks also go to Stuart Morley at Grimley J R Eve who kindly read the text and queried some of my wilder statements. But without the patience, editing skills and support of my wife Patricia this text would be completely unpublishable.

Finally it is necessary to state that this book remains my own work, for good or bad, and not the views of the partners at Richard Ellis, whom I acknowledge and thank for their tolerance.

Preface

Over the last half century many towns and cities have continued to lose residents. Employment has diminished in town centres and many retailers have increasingly chosen out-of-town locations. What is the future of towns and cities in a mature economy like Great Britain?

Since I studied economics in the late 1960s I have worked within and watched the property market of Great Britain change. During the 1970s, an era of high inflation, property investment was perceived as a 'hedge against inflation'. In reality this was a fallacy; in the short term it did not hold true, while in the longer term property was no more a hedge against inflation than investing in stock market equities or purchasing government bonds. Yet property investors and town planners have been caught up in a succession of waves of property market activity which few anticipated or fully understood.

Roger Bootle, in his book *The Death of Inflation*, suggested that inflation may be a thing of the past. If this is true, and if the cyclical patterns of the British Economy and its property market are to be diminished in the future, property investors will have to readdress, in greater detail, the needs of occupiers. They will no longer be able to pretend that their investment decisions are a hedge against inflation, nor in the longer term will inflationary growth be able to hide their investment mistakes.

In recent years I have made a large number of presentations, often on a weekly basis, to investment and property occupier clients, academics and friends addressing the issue of where the property investment market is heading. What will property investment returns be in the years to come, and how will they compare with other forms of investment?

This continually raises questions in my mind, and in those who listen to my presentations of who will want to occupy investment buildings in the future. What are the forces at work changing the property market? What are our politicians and our town planners doing to maintain a vibrant property market such that investors are prepared to invest in the urban environment for the future – particularly in our town and city centres?

These are some of the questions I have attempted to address and answer in this book. As I was putting my thoughts together it occurred to me that very few investors or politicians think deeply about the long-term future of our built environment. Five years is a long time in the world of an investment board or political party. Technology has always played a part but is increasingly having an input on urban land use. Increasing global competition will punish the inefficient cities. Urban efficiency is far more than property rents and capital values. Transport infrastructure and the quality of life of towns and cities has a growing part to play.

This book addresses all these and many other issues and suggests a strategy for developers and investors in the property market; it also addresses some of the issues which should concern politicians and town planners at both local and national level. This book is not a detailed discussion of the intricacies of the town and country planning system or of the details of housing policy. There are numerous books which consider the minutiae of urban issues and far too few which discuss the larger picture. If some of the detail I necessarily refer to is inaccurate, I apologize but hope that any such errors do not blur my central message. My conclusion is that we need a radical shift in strategic thinking in all our towns and cities, ranging from the growing 'stockbroker' towns of the home counties to the older industrial towns and cities outside south-east England.

My hope is that this contribution will play a small part in saving our towns and cities from the ravages of dereliction to both the human spirit and the urban fabric.

Angus McIntosh
London, December 1996

I believe in the supreme worth of the individual and in his right to life, liberty and the pursuit of happiness.

I believe that every right implies a responsibility; every opportunity, an obligation; every possession, a duty.

I believe that the law was made for man and not man for the law; that government is the servant of the people and not their master . . .

John D. Rockefeller Jr
The Rockefeller Center, New York City

Introduction

This is a book about the changing demands placed upon the urban environment in Great Britain. It is a book which attempts (a) to identify some of the major structural changes taking place in the national and international economy, and (b) to discuss these implications for town centres and inner cities. It will also be observed that I have repeated themes that have been covered in articles and conference papers in recent years.

The book is not intended to be a detailed discussion of Town and Country Planning Law, or an analysis of urban design; there are others far more qualified than I to approach the subject of towns and cities from these perspectives. While the subject of 'environmental sustainability' is referred to, the book is more concerned with the socio-economic trends that are shaping our future.

Chapter 1, 'The forces of change and the intransigence of ignorance', discusses how financial deregulation, corporate change and information technology have been largely ignored by mainstream economic discussions. Neither Keynesian nor Monetarist economic theory satisfactorily provides an understanding of these forces currently at work. This lack of awareness at both a national and local level is allowing the forces of the market to dictate the shape of our towns and cities.

Chapter 2, 'Population change yet more counter urbanization?', reviews the pattern of residential decline and growth of urban areas over the last 50 years. These numerical changes are examined from a socio-economic prospective and clearly show that the imbalance between affluent towns and the less affluent inner city areas continues. The suggestion is proposed that we need a new agenda; we should aim to correct the imbalance by encouraging middle income residential development to return to our town and city centres.

Chapter 3, 'Technology: the catalyst to urban change', discusses how the advance of technology has been a recurring theme over the centuries. All urban areas are a product, to some extent, of the application of technological change.

The technology of building materials and transport systems is now giving way to Information Technology as the dominant influencing technology of the late twentieth century.

Chapter 4, 'The spending zone for affluence?', reviews how retail expenditure has dramatically influenced the shape of towns and cities as we know them. It also examines how, particularly during the last decade, the power of retailing has moved away from town and city centres. The suggestion is made that the last half century, with an intensification of retail spend in city centres, is unique in the history of urban development. Never again will retail spending be concentrated into such tight geographic areas. Towns and cities have to face the future; alternative uses for towns and city centres must be found if they are to avoid problems arising from urban dereliction.

Chapter 5, 'Cities: if not for work, then for what?', reviews how employment patterns have altered and are still changing. It provides an outlook to how employment patterns are likely to develop in the next century. This analysis is followed by a review of a number of surveys conducted among office occupiers to examine how they see the future. Planning policy, with reference to the transport infrastructure of urban areas, has failed to understand the needs of business occupiers. A number of commentators have speculated on the nature of work and the future of cities; these provide pointers to the future of town and city centres as locations for employment. However, the impact of these changes has already been significant on the performance of office buildings as investments. The outlook for the office investment sector is very different to the inflationary decades which have recently passed.

Chapter 6, 'The future of cities in an epoch of growing global competition', which is based upon a paper given at an international conference at Cambridge University in 1996, provides an insight into how cities across the world are changing. These stresses and strains of urban development in Great Britain are not unique; they are being experienced in a number of other mature cities around the world. However, it is the rampant growth of cities in Asia and the increasing competition they have created which is likely to change the pecking order of global affluence in the next century.

Chapter 7, 'Property investment and its influence on urban change', provides a review of the property investment market and of the vast amount of data and information generally which is nowadays available. The chapter reviews the recent history of property as an investment vehicle but also corrects a number of the myths about a property, such as: Has property been a good hedge against inflation? What is the outlook for property investment in an era of low inflation?

Chapter 8, 'Strategies for the future', provides a review of a number of issues covered earlier in the book; it is an *aide-memoire* of the forces of change. The chapter then looks at strategies from two different perspectives: the strategies which town and city centre managers need to adopt are subtly different to the approach which should be adopted by property developers and investors in the twenty-first century. However, one set of strategies is a mirror image of the other; town and city centres which are poorly managed will neither attract investment nor compete and survive successfully into the next millennium.

CHAPTER 1
The forces of change and the intransigence of ignorance

Fundamental changes in national economies across the world are having an increasing impact on the future of cities. There is growing evidence that market forces, and their impact on land use, are accelerating the decline of many mature towns and cities. The demand from alternative land uses alone generated by natural market forces may not be sufficient to arrest this decline. In other locations there is excessive demand for land and new development. A significant number of developers and investors in urban property, together with politicians and urban planners, continue to indulge in reflex reactions to these changes, rather than fully examine, understand and implement policies which anticipate these trends. At the end of the twentieth century, towns and cities should be seen as businesses, yet how many towns and cities have a coherent strategic business plan?

In 1970 Alvin Toffler prophetically wrote a book entitled *Future Shock*. He argued that: 'Unless man quickly learns to control the rate of change in his personal affairs, as well as society at large, we are doomed to a massive adaptation breakdown.' As the years pass since Toffler first published his book, we have become increasingly aware that we are in the eye of a hurricane of economic change. There are three dominant forces affecting economies throughout the world which have accelerated the need for greater competitiveness and improved productivity, which, in turn, are having an impact on urban change.

Financial deregulation swept across the world over the last two decades. It started in the mid 1970s in New York with the government removing restrictions on financial organizations and their movement of capital, both nationally and internationally. Financial deregulation came to the City of London in the mid-1980s and has now moved to other countries across the world; towns, cities and countries now compete for finance and investment monies.

Corporate change has also accelerated over the last decade in both the public and private sectors. In the public sector this has been epitomized by the privatization of corporations previously 'owned by the taxpayer'. Great Britain pioneered much of this change with the privatization of assets including council houses, public utilities and transport systems. In parallel with this privatization programme, there has been a programme of corporate change in the private sector: emanating from the United States of America during the recession of the early 1990s, corporate re-engineering, downsizing and delayering (the process of removing a strata of management) have now become catch phases.

As will be discussed in Chapter 5, both financial regulation and corporate change have created increasing pressure for competition, but this competition has been accelerated by a third dominant influence. *Information technology* has now become so influential in the lives of individuals, corporations and governments that it is impossible to ignore. Referring to technology generally, Toffler prophetically said in 1970:

> Advancing technology tends to lower the cost of manufacturing more rapidly than the cost of repair . . . since we can anticipate further technological advance. More improvements coming at ever shorter inter-vals, it often makes hard economic sense to build for the short term rather than the long term . . . as change accelerates and reaches into more and more remote corners of the society, uncertainty about future needs increases. Recognising the inevitability of change, but unsure to the demands it will impose on us, we hesitate to commit large resources for rigidly fixed objects intended to serve unchanging purposes.

A full generation after Toffler made this comment, many towns and cities remain hesitant to seriously plan ahead. Rather than anticipate urban needs 25 years from now, towns and cities are being swept along by the impact of technology. In 1993 Professor Patrick Minford of Liverpool University echoed this theme when he said: 'Technologies which once took decades to transfer to poorer countries can now be instantly transferred through multinationals.'

The impact of technology in areas of the globe previously called the Third World is dramatic. Towns and cities in Great Britain are competing for jobs with these emerging countries. Here in essence is the problem with the growing use of computers and information technology. Towns and cities around the world, in particular in the mature countries such as Great Britain, will change out of recognition over the next 50 years, but most towns and cities are not yet prepared for this change; they do not have a coherent strategy for the future.

In 1961 Jane Jacobs published her famous book *The Death and Life of Great American Cities* and drew attention to the failure of city planning and rebuilding policy in mature cities of America. Jacobs said: 'This book is an attack on current city planning and rebuilding . . . on the principles and aims that have shaped modern, orthodox city planning.' Although this text was widely read and praised, very little appears to have changed. Perhaps this was because the recommendations which Jacobs called 'Different Tactics' were unrealistic or difficult to implement practically.

The polarization of wealth within cities remains; urban decay has continued (and in some cases accelerated) and the impasse of city and town planners to solve urban issues is no different after more than 35 years. My contention is that urban planners at a strategic level continue to address the wrong set of issues, particularly with reference to the economic forces of urban change.

Economic theory and urban change

Economic thinking over the last half century has seen a shift in terms of national economic management. John Maynard Keynes, who died just over 50 years ago, developed his ideas out of the Great Depression of the 1930s, but the high level of unemployment and job insecurity of those times has echoes of what is facing industrialized economies today. Keynes failed to recognize that although there was an economic cyclical problem in the 1920s and the 1930s, there was also a **structural** problem. The growth of the motor car and the use of electricity were already having a technological impact on the need for labour. For instance, telephones, electrified railway systems and the growth of the service sector of the economy were causing significant changes to urban areas before 1939. The interwar period saw the growth of semi-detached suburbia and ribbon development along the new automobile routes, such as the Great West Road on the edge of west London.

In the immediate post-Second World War era, Keynesian economics appeared to answer a number of problems in terms of macro-economic management. However, by the 1970s, doubts began to arise as to whether Keynesian style demand management really had the answer. Keynesian demand management was thought to have contributed to the unnecessary levels of inflation and inefficiency during the first three decades after the war.

From the later 1970s, the pendulum then swung towards the Monetarist view of economic management, which suggested that, rather than Keynesian style 'demand' management, economies should be controlled by 'supply side' management. This school of thought suggests that lower inflation and greater efficiency (and hence wealth generation) will come from controlling not the demand but the supply of money in an economy. In other words, government should not tell people how to spend their money (or spend it for them) but provide the right conditions for individual and corporate preferences. However, the monetary theory was welded to Keynesian thinking in some respects. An example was the supposed link between unemployment and wage or price inflation. This was developed into the 'Philips Curve' concept of economic management, suggesting that there was a trade-off; government could choose higher unemployment or allow greater inflation. However, over time both high unemployment and high inflation ensued, suggesting that the link was not a simple trade-off between these two targets.

By the end of the 1970s Great Britain (and a number of other countries) had entered a period of 'stagflation', an era of high inflation with low economic growth, plus an unacceptably high level of unemployment. Keynesian economics fell into greater disregard, yet there was no deep thinking about urban economics, despite the fact that the majority of people worked in urban areas. There is still no clear link between economic theory and technological/structural change. By the 1980s the disillusionment with Keynesian economics became a political creed. This became a theme in the Mais Lecture given by the

Chancellor of the Exchequer in 1984. As Nigel Lawson (now Lord Lawson) reflects in *The View from No. 11*:

> Instead of seeking to use macro (i.e. fiscal and monetary) policy to promote growth and micro policy (of which income policy was a key component) to suppress inflation, the government should direct macro economic policy to the suppression of inflation and rely on micro economic (or supply side) policy, such as tax and labour market reform, to provide the conditions favourable to improve performance in terms of growth and employment.

In other words, by implication, Nigel Lawson believed that a shift towards a monetary policy would enable urban areas to behave more efficiently as they changed structurally, adapted to new technology and, over the longer term, become generators of wealth. Yet the 1980s was also the decade of significant public expenditure indirectly and directly through Enterprise Zones and Urban Development Corporations. The mainly esoteric discussion between Keynesian economics and Monetary economic theory has rarely, if ever, begun to address the problems of structural change within society, and in particular the impact of technology on urban change, which is a theme that I will develop in greater detail later.

In the Liverpool Investment Letter dated July 1996, Professor Patrick Minford suggested that:

> Too much stabilisation policy can damage your wealth, particularly when it is strongly biased one way or the other. Post-Keynesian policy tried to scotch recessions and is vilified. Post-Monetarist policy is trying to scotch expansion; its exponents should be kept awake by the vilification they too may come to endure.

At the heart of much discussion has been such concepts as NAIRU, or the non-accelerating inflation rate of unemployment. The suggestion has been made that there is a natural rate of unemployment which prevents inflation moving out of control. Such discussion has rarely addressed the structural and geographical impact of such a policy. It appears to have ignored the fact that some geographical areas may have less than 5% unemployment, yet others suffer more than 20% unemployment. Inevitably, it has been the inner urban areas which have had the highest unemployment. In other words, national economic policy has done little if anything to solve the growing problem of urban decline.

Urban decline is closely linked to the application of technological change, yet it is extraordinary to reflect that economic theory has almost totally ignored this fact. The growth of affluence, the accumulation of monetary wealth, the improvements in material standards of living and the increase in leisure time are all products of the application of technology in our lives. The impact it has had on structural change will be discussed later in Chapter 3.

The wealth of towns and cities

So, what is a town or city worth? If you bought the town or city in which you live, how much would you pay for it? One of the anomalies of national and local economic analysis is that it is primarily concerned with cash flow; tax revenue and public expenditure.

In 1967 Professor J.R.S. Revell wrote a book entitled *The Wealth of the Nation*, one of the rare attempts to value government wealth. It is a concept which, even if attempted at a theoretical level, could alter thinking. One might attempt to value both physical property as well as intellectual property (including the quality of education in the population). From the point of view of urban economics, is an urban area gaining in value or diminishing? Without considering such an exercise it is rather like creating a set of company accounts which includes a profit and loss statement without including a balance sheet of assets and liabilities. But that is how the public sector accounts are operated at both a local and national level, until, that is, public assets are privatized. A new procedure is then suddenly adopted, and the value of the assets becomes important in assessing the worth of the organization.

Structural change caused by technological development is an integral part of the changing capital worth of all towns and cities. In the June 1996 *Economic Outlook* from the Organization for Economic Cooperation and Development it was stated that:

> The economies of the OECD are becoming increasingly integrated as a result of technological development and of large increases in flows of international trade, financial capital and foreign direct investment. Many economies in the non OECD are also maturing and their role in international trade and finance is growing rapidly. These developments – which have been described by the term 'globalisation' – will continue to have far reaching implications for economic policy ... Across OECD regions, structural reform has become increasingly important for meeting the challenges proposed by slow output and productivity growth and unacceptably high unemployment rates. Macro economic policies have been able to respond only imperfectly to these problems and, in many cases, the freedom to manoeuvre has been constrained by past excesses or political considerations.

In other words, the OECD is recognizing that technology and the flows of international trade and finance are having an uneven impact. Some areas are benefiting while others are not. National economic policy is frequently failing to recognize or adjust to the impact of 'globalization'.

> By insuring sustainable long term growth, macro economic policy can facilitate structural reforms. At the same time, structural reforms are needed to enhance growth prospects, create jobs and ensure higher living standards.

But it is a failure to identify appropriate 'structural reforms' which results in such uneven geographic economic activity. At present many inner urban areas are in decline, while some outer urban areas are prospering.

The town planners, the economists and the politicians

Managing urban change has largely been left to the discipline of 'urban planning', but the central mistake of urban planning has been to concentrate on

5

physical planning, with very little understanding of the economics of structural change, and arguably to misuse the word 'planning'. While the intentions have without doubt been laudable, much town and country 'planning' has not been able to 'plan' urban change. In 1947 the British Parliament passed the famous Town and Country Planning Act, a revolutionary and visionary all-embracing piece of legislation concerned with urban change. It should perhaps have been called 'The Urban and Rural Land Management Controls Act', with an emphasis on management control. In other words, this Act of Parliament and successive acts of parliament, have not fully understood the economic forces of change which have radically (in some cases devastatingly) changed urban areas in Great Britain over the last 50 years.

To plan, according to a dictionary definition, implies a statement of 'intention, a way of proceeding'. It is economic market forces which cause change, not the town planning system. To use a football metaphor, the manager of the game has been money financing urban development. The players on the pitch have been the investors, developers, architects and occupiers of buildings. The town planner has been the referee, aided and abetted by his assistants (linesmen) who have blown the whistle from time to time, calling offside or foul.

A lack of understanding of the forces of economic change has been illustrated by the various attempts to nationalize land values. Over the post-1945 period we have seen the introduction of the Betterment Levy and, following its failure, the Development Gains Tax and its revised version the Development Land Tax. All these attempts to tax land value have failed, not so much as a result of political pressure but out of a lack of awareness of their impact on urban land development. The lack of understanding of urban areas has not improved.

Although the planning system may have failed to understand the economic forces of change, the 1947 Act and subsequent statutes have created much which is of benefit. These range from a framework of Building Regulations at the micro-building level, to Green Belts and National Parks – an issue pioneered by Barbara Castle MP in 1947 with her drive to open the country to the majority – at the macro-regional level of planning. However, the last two decades have tried to come to terms with the fact that there is 'no such thing as a free lunch'. All public benefits have to be paid for by wealth created in a market economy.

The drive to create wealth is a theme developed by Will Hutton in *The State We're In*. He suggests: 'Not merely the economy, but society has been "marketized" – with an increase in anxiety, dread of the future and communal breakdown'. This discussion of economic theory between individual freedom versus control has also recently been highlighted by Lord Robert Skidelsky in his polemic *The World after Communism*, where he suggests:

> The great ideological struggle of the 20th century has been between collectivism and liberalism. Collectivism was defined . . . as government for the good of the people by experts or officials who know or think they know what is good for the people, better than the non official person or the mass of people themselves. . . . Liberalism had two aims . . . the first

was to release the individual from social fetters; the second was to disperse power.

This discussion between 'collectivism' and 'liberalism' seems to have passed by what has actually been happening in the economics of urban locations. Buckminster Fuller, the designer and philosopher, once described New York as a:

> Continual evolutionary process of evaluations, demolitions, removals, temporary vacant lots, new installations and repeat. . . . Most people look upon the building operations blocking New York streets . . . as temporary annoyances, soon to disappear into the static peace. They still think of permanence as normal, a hangover from the Newtonian view of the universe. But those who have lived in and with New York since the beginning of the century have literally experienced living with Einsteinian relativity.

This continual process of urban change has swung from 'command given' urban development in many countries in the early decades after the Second World War, to 'market driven' forces of change in the last decade. The horror of town council expenditure on concrete high rise housing in some areas has gone, to be replaced by the competitive market forces of urban change, not only in Britain but across the world.

Do we have the correct agenda for managing urban change?

Urban change will always be with us and has been with us since the beginning of civilization. In the late twentieth century – in addition to the impact of financial deregulation, corporate change and information technology – two factors are accelerating this process of change: first, the growing urbanization of the world's population and, second, the increasing rate of decay of older cities. Approximately 50% of the world's population of 6 billion people are currently living in urban areas, and by the second decade of the next century, this figure will have risen to almost 70%. The change in urbanization is illustrated by the United Nations statistics on the five largest cities (Tables 1.1 and 1.2).

In 1995 only 83 cities in the world had a population over 1 million; by 2015 over 500 cities with greater than one million inhabitants will exist. It is estimated that nine-tenths of the world's population will grow in the urban

City	Residents (millions)
1. New York	12.3
2. London	8.7
3. Tokyo	6.9
4. Paris	5.4
5. Moscow	5.4

Source: United Nations.

Table 1.1 Global largest cities 1950

7

City	Residents (millions)
1. Tokyo	28.7
2. Bombay	27.4
3. Lagos	24.4
4. Shanghai	23.4
5. Jakarta	21.2

Table 1.2 Global largest cities 2015

Source: United Nations.

areas of developing countries. Half of the population increase will be attributable due to the growth of population generally and the other half to the continuing mass migration into cities.

The enormous growth of cities is characterised by the twin problems of growing poverty and growing affluence. Both are increasing the levels of pollution and destitution, yet some of the worst levels of poverty are to be found in the mature cities of America and Europe. The UN agency, The International Labour Organization, is calling for greater efforts to create jobs for the growing number of urban poor.

Urbanization is also having a dramatic impact on the world's resources. It is estimated that cities currently occupy 2% of the world's land surface yet use some 75% of the world's resources and release similar percentages of waste. It is further estimated that the demand for energy in the next 25 years will have increased to 88% higher than the 1990 level.

There has been considerable discussion regarding this issue and the concept of sustainable development in recent years. It has been suggested that there is an 'ecological imperative' to review issues such as population size, forms of agriculture, bio-diversity, energy consumption, global warming as well as urban conservation. It has further been suggested that dense urban areas are, according to Jenks, Burton and Williams in *The Compact City*, not just a great attraction 'to architects, planners and urban designers, but to countless tourists'. However, I would argue that it is the forces of the market – that is, the actions of the individuals and corporations – which are determining the future land use, dense or otherwise. The forces of the market are very powerful, as I witnessed in the early years of the 1990s in central and eastern Europe following the collapse of the Soviet Union. In the absence of clear laws and urban guidance, office development appeared in the most unlikely place, sometimes with extremely high rents. In Budapest, for instance, telephone technology, some of which dated from 1938, dictated office location; the east side of the River Dunube had a better system than the west and hence attracted most international office occupiers. The shortage of supply forced rents up to extraordinarily high levels. The wholesale privatization within the Soviet empire heightened the need for food, clothing, housing and jobs. The attractions of compact or less compact urban form was, and is, far less important to many.

Jenks, Burton and Williams, and other contributors such as Michael Breheny, have included a discussion of the concept of decentralized cities versus compact urban areas: Which is the more sustainable? In the last half century market forces in the mature economics have created greater decentralization. In the younger economies cities have expanded with great compactness, sometimes referred to as being overcrowded. It is far from clear which type of urban form is more or less sustainable in terms of its environmental impact. The UN Conference on Environment and Development in Rio de Janeiro in 1992 set out principles for achieving sustainable development, despite the problem of measuring such a concept. The simple reality is that greater affluence creates the desire for greater travel and other leisure activities which may not be sustainable in the long term, but tackling the problem at a local level may be impractical, as towns, cities and regions, in an increasingly competitive world, are almost powerless.

The issue of environmental sustainability can only be tackled at a national or international level. Carbon taxes, emission regulations (for vehicles and power stations) and statutes relating to thermal insulation or the dumping of waste are likely to have a far higher impact than physical urban development restrictions. Physical land use constraints, as well as problems associated with land contamination and the creation of an Environmental Agency (as in Great Britain), may have the reverse impact, accelerate urban decline and make cities less sustainable.

Urban stress

In the mature countries of the world, including Great Britain, most of Europe and the United States of America, structural change is having a different impact to that of the growing cities of Asia; it appears to be accelerating the process of urban decline. In almost all towns and cities across Great Britain it is possible to identify a growing number of empty buildings, an increasing level of urban poverty and, possibly linked to both of these, an increasing level of urban crime. The cost of crime is an increasing burden on many countries making them less efficient in a competitive marketplace. The costs of insurance, policing, vandalism as well as penal institutions are rising. As Stephen Shaw in 'A bull market for prisons' in *The World in 1997* has observed: 'More people will be locked up in prison in 1997 than ever before. The expense will be so great that taxpayers may soon start to complain.'

Table 1.3 illustrates the cost to urban society. Almost one person per thousand inhabitants in England and Wales is being paid for in prison.

While it has to be acknowledged that the prison population may be rising due to more crime being reported or to a higher rate of detection and

Netherlands	55
Sweden	66
Germany	83
England & Wales	96
Spain	106
USA	387
Russia	443

Source: Council for Europe, Prison Reform Trust/*The World in 1997*, The Economist

Table 1.3 Imprisonment per 100 000 population

prosecution, the cost of crime is a factor influencing urban change and deferring investment. As Geraldine Pettersson observes in 'Crime and mixed use development' in *Reclaiming the City*, it is now 25 years since Oscar Newman defined the concept of 'defensible space' and gave three factors which made crime easy to commit (impersonal areas, lack of natural surveillance and poor design visibility).

Despite CCTV in many city centres, the overall cost of crime is higher than in 1972. However, by tackling minor offences, New York has recently cut its overall rate of crime. Since its peak in 1990 all crime has fallen by more than 70% and the number of murders is also down by almost the same percentage. Business management principles in the New York Police Department have reduced crime.

Investors, developers and occupiers of real estate are increasingly aware of this process of change. Equally, if the process is to be amended and cities in the economically mature world are to be made efficient and more capable of competing across the world, politicians at both a local and national level need to wake up to the issue of global change. For instance, two recent surveys have attempted to give competitiveness scores for a number of countries. The World Economic Forum (WEF) Global Competitiveness Report in 1996 placed Luxembourg as the most competitive European country, yet the International Institute of Management Development (IMD) in Lausanne placed Denmark in the same year at number one. Both studies placed Russia, where crime has been rising and there is a very high prison population, as the least competitive. The main issue is not whether one report is better, or more accurate, than the other. The fact that either report was produced is significant; the global economy nowadays places great emphasis on productivity and efficiency generally. Understanding the role of cities, in this new world trend towards 'benchmarking' efficiency, is crucial.

Politicians are increasingly aware of the problem. In *Planning for Prosperity* in 1996, Keith Vaz, the New Labour Shadow Minister for Urban Affairs, suggested: 'A reinvigorated and more efficient planning system would greatly help local government deliver its new agenda to promote the social, economic and environmental well-being of the communities they serve.' Such sentiments are fine, but will they work? If urban regeneration is to work it may also be insufficient, as the Conservative government said in 1995: 'Local governments must now be given the opportunity to provide real civic leadership and build creative local partnerships if we are to find solutions to the problems to urban Britain.'

Is it sufficient for politicians to discuss 'reinventing the city' and glibly talk about 'cities as centres of opportunity' as New Labour said in its 1996 document *Reinventing the City*? Government departments have also issued statements such as there should be 'an emphasis on a plan-led approach to promoting developments in town centres' and the 'promotion of mixed used development and retention of key town centre uses . . .'. These appear in the Department of the Environment's Consultation Paper *Planning Policy Guidance Note 6* of July 1995, but they imply a lack of awareness of the real issues. The Consultation Paper; *Planning Policy Guidance Note 1* (Revised) dated July 1996 says it 'reaffirms the role of the planning system in meeting the needs of a growing and competitive economy . . .'. But we know from experience over the last 50 years that the planning system on its own cannot deliver this role.

In a speech given at Canary Wharf in September 1996, referring to the enormous changes in retailing, Keith Vaz highlighted the old dilemma. With echoes of Nicholas Ridley, a former Conservative Secretary of State for the Environment during the Margaret Thatcher years of the 1980s, he said: 'Whitehall should not stand in the way of the retail revolution.' Yet, in the same speech, Keith Vaz addressed one of the tactical issues of town planning which has dominated urban development for over half a century, at the expense of understanding the larger strategic issues changing urban areas. He said: 'The message to us about planning gain has been simple. There must be clear and consistent rules and complete transparency. We shall ensure that we have them.'

As we all know, planning gains are a quasi tax on development, but what if the forces of change mean there are no development proposals in the first place? If the history of the last 50 years tells us nothing else, it says that physical 'town planning' has largely failed at a strategic level. It has neither anticipated nor prevented the decline of town centres. It has also continually been unable to plan for the forces of change and has not been able to harness the forces of the market. Political and financial power has slowly disappeared for many towns and cities. Charles Handy, in *The Empty Raincoat*, has summed up the change:

> There used, in Britain, to be a thing called civic pride. Town hall would compete with town hall in magnificence and in achievement. Central government down the decades has progressively stripped cities and towns of their powers, distrustful of how they used those powers and, in some cases, undoubtedly abused them. All that is left in Britain of this tradition is the city football club.

Although there has been an on-going discussion within Europe with regard to Federalism and the principle of subsidiarity, financial power in Great Britain is still centrally controlled. Subsidiarity is the principle that responsibility and decisions should be pushed as far out of and down the organization as possible. Many of the more successful urban areas in Britain over the last half century have been the New Towns and Urban Development Corporations. In these locations political powers, legal powers, financial powers and physical planning powers have all been brought together. Combining these powers within local or regional government, such as at Cardiff Bay, may be a model for all urban areas in the future, not just for those pockets within urban areas with the greatest need.

In *Third Millennium Management* Peter Martin has suggested that most formal management theories are founded on costs. Outsourcing, downsizing, re-engineering and many other theories fall into this category. *Third Millennium Management* replaces these ideas by putting revenue–generation at the heart of strategy. If local government were able to apply this simple objective and increase revenue, the management of towns and cities would achieve positive results.

This is the agenda for the future; as I will discuss in Chapter 7, the private investment market needs greater clarity from the public sector. The new agenda therefore requires greater certainty in terms of legal, financial and physical powers at a local and regional level. If these factors are not combined the forces of the market will continue to leave urban dereliction in its wake.

CHAPTER 2

Population change yet more counter-urbanization?

The residential populations of all towns and cities are always changing; they may be expanding or contracting, becoming more youthful or ageing, or changing in terms of their socio-economic composition. Over time these changes become reflected in the way towns and cities use their land. As E.F. Schumacher stated in *Small is Beautiful*: 'Among material resources, the greatest, unquestionably, is the land. Study how society uses its land, and you can come to pretty reliable conclusions as to what its future will be.'

The computerization of demographic information nowadays provides both investors in the private sector, as well as administrators in the public sector, with a useful tool to understand land in urban areas. However, as will be discussed in Chapter 7, as an aid to more enlightened town planning (or urban management), there is very little evidence that this data has been used successfully in strategic planning.

Population change

The last half century has been characterized by a continuing process of counter-urbanization. Generally the larger cities have continued to lose population – a phenomenon which has been common in many mature economies. Between 1961 and 1991, inner London lost more than one million residents, a quite staggering decrease. Manchester and Liverpool have both experienced larger percentage declines, but even combining these two cities together, the number of people who migrated outwards is still less than the decline in the number of residents in inner London.

Over the same 30-year period, Glasgow has shown the largest decline, a drop of 43%, while Edinburgh has seen nearly a quarter of its population disappear. With the exception of inner London, the statistics show that the real acceleration in urban population decline took place after 1971; only inner

	1961	1971	1981	1991	Decline 1961–91
Inner London	3492	3031	2497	2343	-33%
Outer London	4499	4420	4215	4050	-10%
Birmingham	1183	1097	1006	937	-21%
Manchester	662	543	448	400	-40%
Liverpool	745	610	509	449	-40%
Leeds	712	738	704	676	-5%
Newcastle upon Tyne	336	308	277	264	-21%
Cardiff	289	287	273	277	-4%
Glasgow	1140	982	765	653	-43%
Edinburgh	483	476	436	421	-23%

Table 2.1 Examples of declining cities ('000s)

Source: ONS, National Census.

London had shown a significant fall in population in the previous decade. Some of the cities in decline since 1961 are listed in Table 2.1.

It was Dr David Eversley who first drew attention to this problem. Having dramatically reshaped the Greater London Development Plan for the Greater London Council in the late 1960s, Eversley noted that there were some significant changes taking place in the structure of London. In 1973, with David Donnison, he published a book *London, Urban Patterns, Problems and Policies* which began to change the direction of British urban policy, recognizing that an inner city problem existed and that it had structural roots in the changing urban economy. Eversley pointed out what is now commonplace but was then shocking 'that London, then seen as the golden corner of Britain, was heading into deep economic waters'. This was the point made by Professor Peter Hall in his obituary of David Eversley in 1995, but despite bringing this economic perspective into the minds of planners, urban planning has not changed significantly over approximately the past 20 years. The decline of the population in larger urban areas has been reflected in the growth of a number of smaller towns, districts or parts of larger conurbations around Great Britain (Table 2.2).

From this example of towns that have grown significantly over the last 30 years, it is not surprising that the top two are post-Second World War 'New Towns'. The concept of building new towns gained momentum throughout the nineteenth and early twentieth century with a number of enlightened housing developments pointing the way, such as Bournville near Birmingham, Port Sunlight near Liverpool and Letchworth Garden City (founded on the ideas of Ebernezer Howard). The new town movement started officially with the New Towns Act of 1946, as Frank Schaffer says in *The New Town Story*:

> The aim of most of the New Towns is to relieve pressure on over crowding in the big cities such as London, Birmingham, Liverpool, Manchester or Glasgow. For social and economic reasons the site of the

	1961	1971	1981	1991	Increase 1961–91
Bracknell	43	64	82	94	118%
Milton Keynes	49	66	124	173	253%
Guildford	108	118	120	122	13%
Solihull	128	192	198	196	53%
Bromsgrove	64	77	88	90	40%
Bury	151	174	176	173	15%
Chester-le-Street	43	48	52	52	21%
Vale of Glamorgan	90	102	110	111	23%
Bearsden/Milngavie	26	36	40	40	54%
West Lothian	86	111	138	141	64%

Source: ONS, National Census.

Table 2.2 Examples of growing towns ('000s)

New Town must be within a reasonable distance away – not too near to be in danger of coalescing, destroying green belts or encouraging commuting; not too far away to destroy commercial and industrial ties or split up families too much.

Social structure and inner cities

It is ironic that the New Towns movement, born out of socio/political good will, should have accelerated the decline of many urban areas and accelerated the 'inner city' problem which we know today. The current inner city problem is illustrated by Table 2.3. Town A is situated in south-east England, Town B is situated adjacent to a major urban area outside south-east England.

Town A has an age profile not dissimilar to the profile for Great Britain, although there is a slightly higher percentage in the working age group (age 20–54). The ethnic origin of the population in Town A is also very similar to the Great Britain average but it is clear that the distribution of social class is biased towards the professional/managerial/skilled end of the spectrum. Perhaps not surprisingly there are more households with two or more cars, compared with the national average. Town B has a disproportionately high number of young people (under the age of 20) and its population of the ethnic Indian sub-continent group and the Black category are above the national average. There is a far lower percentage of professional/managerial/skilled individuals compared with the national average, yet a far higher percentage of manual or semi-skilled individuals. Also, perhaps not surprisingly, a high percentage (more than a third) of the households do not have access to a car. Town A and Town B illustrate the problem of residential Great Britain in the late twentieth century. Despite the laudable Town and Country Planning Act 1947, and numerous amendments and re-enactments since that legislation was passed, urban areas remain unequal in terms of their socio-economic populations. Town A could be (but is not) on the list of growing towns illustrated earlier; Town B falls within one of the urban areas listed as a declining city, also shown earlier.

15

	Town A	Town B	GB average
Resident population: within 20 minutes drive time	830 608	287 829	–
	%	%	%
Age: Under 2	26.3	28.7	25.3
20–54	52.9	46.2	48.3
54+	20.8	25.1	26.4
Ethnic origin:			
White	93.9	77.4	94.5
Black	2.2	6.1	1.6
Indian sub-continent	2.5	14.6	2.7
Chinese	0.3	0.3	0.3
Asian	0.4	0.5	0.4
Other ethnic group	0.7	1.1	0.5
Economically active by social class:			
Professional/Managerial	40.6	22.6	31.7
Skilled non-manual	24.9	22.4	22.6
Skilled manual	17.4	24.5	21
Semi-skilled	10.8	20.3	15.7
Unskilled	4.6	6.2	6.1
On government training scheme	0.5	2.1	1.3
Armed forces/unstated	1.2	1.8	1.6
Private households:			
With no car	16.2	36.4	25.9
With 1 car	40.9	41.7	43.8
With 2 cars	32.9	17.4	23.7
With 3+ cars	10	4.5	6.6

Table 2.3 The inner city problem

Source: Based on CACI Data.

Income inequality

Physical 'town planning' has failed to arrest this change and there is growing evidence that urban societies are becoming even more unequal. In recent years there have been numerous studies on this subject. They are summed up by *The Economist* of 5 November 1994 on the subject of inequality when it was stated:

> Income inequalities in America and Britain are greater than at any time in the past fifty years. The socio consequences of this change worry many. Such concerns make the 1980s seem with hindsight a time of comforting economic simplicity: the job was to cut taxes, trim the role of government, boost incentives and allow markets to work better. The task of the coming decade – discovering how to spread the benefit of economic efficiency more widely – will be far harder.

Inevitably the polarization of wealth, whether it is income or asset wealth, raises important yet difficult political issues. Is the polarization of wealth

Fig. 2.1. Urban dwellings for the underclass at Waterloo, London. Does the greater polarization of income and the growth of the meritocratic élite create greater problems for towns and cities as they compete to survive?

necessary to raise the overall wealth of society? Does a polarization of income raise economic growth? If it does, is economic growth compatible with an improvement in the quality of life (Fig. 2.1), both spiritually and culturally?

The Economist summarized the challenge for town planners. But physical planning alone will not solve the social ills which a more competitive world creates. From the London Borough of Camden to the Toxteth suburb of Liverpool, physical town planning policies need a totally new agenda. Meanwhile, the Department of the Environment has continued to issue consultation notes concerned with town centres, suggesting that there should be the 'promotion of mixed use developments and retention of key town centre uses' and that its consultation paper claims it 'clarifies the relationship between previous planning policy guidance note relating to the transport and retailing'. But do such statements really address the issue?

The meritocratic élite

The subject of inequality is linked to the striving towards a meritocracy. In *The Economist* of 13 July 1996 an article entitled 'The impossible dream?' stated: 'American intellectuals are losing faith in the merits of meritocracy but have little to replace it.' It suggested that the trend towards a meritocracy was widening the gap between rich and poor and that the income of the least well educated had fallen relative to the well educated and that this was worsening the condition of the underclass. *The Economist* then stated:

> That America is pursuing social mobility at the expense of social cohesion and civil virtue is the central claim of 'The Bell Curve'. The bright have retreated to fortified apartment blocks or distant suburbs. The dull live in crime-infested inner cities spawning children and collecting welfare.

The Bell Curve by Richard Herrnstein and Charles Murray caused controversy when first published in 1994 in the USA. It suggested that the best jobs increasingly go to the cognitive élite, those able to benefit from the best schools, rather than those in a particular social class. The underclass, it is suggested, is increasingly formed of those with low intelligence. The study covers the relationship between IQ and crime, race, fertility and social policy. Clearly, the concept of IQ is open to debate but the authors say:

> our thesis is that the twentieth century has continued the transformation, so that the twenty-first will open on a world in which cognitive ability is the driving force. The shift is more subtle than the previous one but more momentous. Social class remains the vehicle of social life, but intelligence now pulls the train.

In the pre-industrial agricultural age the aristocracy were the élite. As the industrial revolution gathered momentum in the nineteenth century, society changed. The industrial élite emerged, for instance in the form of the railway barons and the coal mine owners. In parallel, a new mercantile élite grew, able to trade material goods and finance the industrial society. This middle class, between the old aristocracy and the working class, has grown enormously in the twentieth century with 40% or more of all economic growth originating from the service sector of the economy.

Over the last decade or more a new élite has emerged, including those able to handle information technology in the information age. This new élite is made up of those able to develop hardware and software for the information age, as well as those able to benefit from its application. The City of London and the financial traders, for instance, clearly fall into this second élite subcategory. As will be discussed later, the other élite group in the late twentieth century relates to the growing leisure sector, the entertainment élite ranging from footballers to film stars.

Are the forces of the market economy, combined with the growth of a meritocratic élite and physical town planning policies, making the urban problem worse? Is a new form of meritocratic élite emerging which obeys different land-use criteria to previous generations? T.B. Bottomore in *Elites and Society* suggests that the definition of an élite is a relatively new idea, stemming principally from the nineteenth-century economist, Vilfredo Pareto. Although élite groups existed in previous civilizations, such as the ancient Greeks or Romans, it was Pareto who defined the élite as 'a class of people who have highest indices in their branch of activity'. Pareto suggests there are both governing and non-governing élites. Town planning and its difficulties can be said to be the struggle between the governing élite (the paymasters of town planners) and the non-governing élite (the forces of the land market). It is the lack of understanding of the second group which has partly caused the first group's apparent failure; it rarely understands which land uses are changing and why.

An example of this problem, in the late 1990s, is the need for extra households. With the average size of households falling, it is estimated by the government that an extra 4.4 million houses will be needed in the next 20 years, but an investigation by Breheny and Hall for the Town and Country Planning Association (sponsored by the Joseph Rowntree Foundation) in 1996 concluded: 'Large-scale use of previously undeveloped ''greenfield'' sites is inevitable if the forecast increase in households is to be accommodated.' The report identified a mismatch between demand for housing and land availability, being particularly accute west of London (in the south-east), in Cheshire, in Cumbria, in rural Lancashire (in the north-west) and in north Yorkshire (in the Yorkshire and Humberside region). The report perhaps subconsciously identifies the growing problem of land use in a competitive world market. Land 'shortage' will increasingly appear in those areas where the meritocratic élite want to live, such as in the Thames Valley west of London or in Cheshire, south-west of Manchester. Despite John Gummer, the Secretary of State for the Environment, stating in late 1996 that he wanted to see 60% of the 4.4 million extra households built in existing urban areas, the concept of land-use winners and losers is increasingly apparent nationally and internationally.

But closely linked to the geographic polarization of the population into the meritocratic élite at one end of the spectrum (and its impact on property markets), and the underclass at the other, is the issue of education. J.K. Galbraith discusses education as a prerequisite for *The Good Society*: 'education makes democracy possible, and, along with economic development, it makes it necessary, even inevitable.' Yet we all know that some geographic areas succeed better than others. Those fortunate enough to be able to pay for education can sometimes gain from such expenditure while others pay for education indirectly by moving to geographic catchment areas where education standards and state school reputations are held in high regard.

Robin Morris has recently observed that one-third of British men between the ages of 25 and 64 who were without a job in 1995 were also without educational qualifications. Norman Macrae in an article 'The thieving state' in *The World in 1997* published by *The Economist*, has stated:

> In education we will have to move to some system of vouchers, with voucher payments initially highest for those who set up decently competitive schools in the worst inner cities, where teaching standards and attendance have actually declined in the past 25 years of an extraordinary information revolution which should have hugely increased both.

It is a statement of the obvious that those state schools located within areas of so-called 'social deprivation' – where most of the children may not speak English as a first language, or suffer other social problems – need special help. These sink schools of the underclass geographic areas clearly need smaller classes if those educated are to compete with the meritocratic élite in the more affluent suburbs.

The concept of a group of 10 or thereabouts as the ideal team number has become widely established since Anthony Jay wrote *Corporation Man* in 1972. Jesus had 12 disciples, a jury has 12 members, a hockey, cricket or soccer side has 11 players, a rowing eight contains 9 members including the coxswain and a rugby side contains 15 which is broken into 8 forwards and 7 backs. Meredith Belbin has taken this idea further by discussing the varying roles which different team members play to make the group or tribe collectively successful. It is therefore strange that education has largely ignored a concept widely accepted in management philosophy. Classes frequently contain between 30 and 40 pupils, and occasionally more. This factor, together with a lack of management rigour in some educational establishments, has contributed to the polarization of meritocratic attainment and is reflected in the property markets of our towns and cities as they compete to survive.

Bottomore quotes Pareto, saying 'history is the graveyard of aristocracies', suggesting that there is a constant 'circulation of élites' which involves individuals entering or leaving élite groups, or may involve élite groups rising and declining. There is no doubt that, in whatever form, the middle-income élite are an important element of balance in urban residential land development.

Over a number of decades a confused agenda has appeared in connection with these issues and many proposals have been sugested to rebuild the urban fabric of Great Britain. One particular project, which could have been the largest urban regeneration project in Europe, illustrates the issues.

King's Cross – a residential planning problem

In 1987 the British Railways Board invited, within a matter of weeks, tenders for a site of 120 acres of land to the north of King's Cross Station in London (Fig. 2.2). Over the previous year the London Regeneration Consortium had been discussing this site with British Rail, but it was correctly felt that the ideas should be put out to both a design and a financial tender. In the few weeks allocated by the tender, Speyhawk Plc came up with an innovative proposal, neatly dividing the site into three parts: The front section would involve an underground rail station linking with the Channel Tunnel (part of the planning brief). Above this station would be office buildings and a hotel. The middle

Fig. 2.2. King's Cross. Over 100 acres of land remains largely vacant, one of the largest city centre regeneration sites in Europe, suitable for mixed use development including middle-income housing.

section of the site would be a mixture of refurbished community buildings facing onto the Grand Union Canal, but also involving some business space offices and a retailing area. The third area of the site would be concerned with industrial/workspace development and residential development. In the event British Rail decided to stay with the London Regeneration Consortium's proposal and there then ensued a discussion, which lasted more than three years, with the town planners of two local authorities, plus other legally involved parties. Throughout these three years or more there were conflicts between the London Borough of Camden and the London Borough of Islington. The whole of the British Rail site lay within the London Borough of Camden yet all the principal road access routes to and from the site passed over land within the boundary of the London Borough of Islington.

One of the hottest debated issues related to the Social Housing Nomination Rights as one of the principal planning gains. By 1992 the project had been abandoned; the national and London economy was in recession, property values had fallen dramatically and there was no obvious demand for the office buildings which would have provided the principal value to justify the extremely high development costs. At no time during more than five years of discussion did the two London Boroughs appear to seriously consider the housing element of the site for anything other than Social Housing. Although middle-income private housing was proposed in the scheme, this was generally tolerated rather than applauded (Fig. 2.3). Also, very low down on the agenda, was the fact that this site is one of the most environmentally 'transport friendly' locations for dense urban land use anywhere in Europe. It is immediately adjacent to two mainline railway stations and within a short walking distance of another. No less than five underground railway lines pass under the site and it also has the Thames Link surface railway connections. In addition, it is the

Fig. 2.3. King's Cross. The Grand Union Canal behind King's Cross Station would make an ideal setting for mixed use development, including residential use.

21

proposed location for the eventual terminal of the Channel Tunnel high-speed link, connecting Kings Cross with mainland Europe.

Rather than accelerating the planning process and developing a public transport-efficient development, the physical urban planners and local politicians became bogged down in tactical issues, including those concerned with local Social Housing Nomination Rights. By 1995 a proposal called 'King's Cross, A New Quarter for London' had emerged with £37.5 million of funding, to include more than 20 CCTV cameras, less emphasis on office development but an attempt to balance commercial uses to 'enhance London's role as a world city', but also aiming to meet certain social housing and employment objectives.

Promoting social housing

Behind much of the discussion at King's Cross in the 1980s was and is the political debate concerning the appropriate and most effective way to promote social housing. Should it be supply led – in other words, should the public sector provide social housing – or should it be demand led? Should certain sectors of society be assisted financially so that they can afford to buy or rent a reasonable standard of housing? Such housing could be located in a variety of locations, such as within middle-income districts, not clustered into low-income housing zones.

This is one of the issues behind the Housing Act 1996 and the creation of Local Housing Companies. Since 1988 £10.1 bn has been invested in the country's 2200 housing associations providing, with other government grants, over 300 000 new houses. The new Local Housing Companies, combining local authority finance with private finance (a variation of the Private Finance Initiative), may be able to accelerate social housing provision. In December 1996 the Nationwide Building Society announced that it was set to become the first big lender to a local housing company, initially with Rochester–upon–Medway. The 1996, the central government budget also included the announcement of a £70 million, three-year challenge fund aimed at inner city areas. The concern remains; the needs for social housing may continue to be confused with the objective of land use controls and the town planning system.

A recent example of this issue relates to the future of the Parkhill Flats, built like a fortress for lower income families on a hillside outside Sheffield. It was built in the post-Second World War wave of social engineering when Harold Macmillan, the Conservative Prime Minister in the 1950s, and other politicians of all parties aimed to increase the stock of housing in Great Britain. Roy Hattersley, former housing committee Chairman in Sheffield and later deputy leader of the Labour Party, says of Parkhill Flats: 'It seemed a good idea at the time. And I have no doubt that it was Parkhill Flats – now simultaneously excoriated by tenants and awarded listed building status by English Heritage – fulfilled a specific and practical purpose. I am biased about Parkhill. I built it.' But, later, Hattersley concludes: 'Parkhill was built to meet the needs of the people. If it no longer achieves that aim, it should be demolished.'

If there is only one important lesson which we have learnt over the last 50 years it is that physical town planning controls cannot solve the social problems of urban society by simply building more social housing. Building yet more social housing, whether it be high rise or low rise, in an area already containing a social problem, appears to accelerate the process of urban decline.

Referring to Town A and Town B mentioned earlier (see page 16), the target for an urban location such as Town B (which might have been Sheffield or King's Cross) should be to encourage middle-income housing, not to solve the socio-economic problem by creating, or requiring, yet more 'social housing'. Creating 'social housing' in an area already suffering from a high proportion of low-income housing will not address the issue of 'income inequalities' which *The Economist* and others have identified as one of the products of liberalized national economies in a world of greater global competition. Such a policy is likely to increase the geographic polarization of land use between the better off (the meritocratic élite) and the underclass.

Promoting middle-income housing

The issue of reversing the trend and creating middle-income residential development in central London is not new. In the immediate post-Second World War years the development of the Barbican on the northern edge of the City of London epitomized this challenge. Inner and outer central London contained a population of approaching 8 million people in the early decades after the war, similar to the population of a country such as Sweden. Yet its level of unemployment over the years has been similar to the residential population of a town such as Derby. As Judy Hillman in *Planning for London* in 1971 observed: 'As a capital, as the magnet of Europe, as port, as industrial, commercial and travel centre . . . London is Rome, Babylon, Venice and Mecca in one. But London only just works.'

London's problems are complex, partly due to the problems of congestion it creates. Over the years there have been a number of attempts at social–cost/benefit analysis relating to travel time, but none has seriously looked at the concept of developing residential areas in London as a way of reducing travel time and creating social benefits. Nowadays the issues of 'sustainability' and 'mixed use development' have emerged, repackaging the issue into new environment speak.

As Richard Lawton pointed out in 'The journey to work in Britain' more than 25 years ago, there have been two tendencies at work: the concentration of industries and services and the rehousing of people from overcrowded central areas. These two tendencies have not been in harmony. There is no doubt that London as an urban area has continued to suffer from the pressures of agglomeration. Over the past 50 years or more London should have carried out a total reassessment of the role for mixed residential development, to re-address the problem. The editorial of *Macleans*, a Canadian magazine, said in 1971:

> Today's clogged streets, dirty air, sprawling suburbs, the whole planners mess – are steadily making cities less liveable . . . In recent years many Canadians have realized that the quality of a city's life bears no relation to the quantity of concrete. The main objective must constantly be kept in mind, it is not to provide better conditions for vehicles but to revitalize cities . . . How much travelling is really necessary . . . How much travelling is simply a waste of time.

The Barbican success story
The Barbican in the City of London development neatly addressed this issue in its press release in 1970:

> In 1851 nearly 128 000 people lived – somewhat uncomfortably – within the 'square mile' of the City of London, the financial and Mercantile Centre of that technology. A century later the commercial building of the late 19th century, the growth of 'dormitory' suburbs in the wake of rapid railway expansion and the ravages of the blitz, has combined to produce utterly different cities of London; by day, the bustling city of commerce and finance, populated by half a million commuting workers; by night, a ghostly empty precinct of barely 5000 – a City of cats and caretakers.

As mentioned earlier, Dr David Eversley produced interesting statistics in the early 1970s which showed that the combination of planning controls and perhaps the dis-economies of London, were increasing unemployment. Although unemployment levels in London were only 1.6% at that time, this represented nearly 10% of the country's total unemployed. This clearly showed that unemployment in London was becoming far more important than in other parts of the country. David Eversley was able to show that as many as 50 000 jobs had vanished from the London area. He suggested that, by the late 1970s, 128 000 would be unemployed in the London area alone. As we know, the number increased well beyond this figure by the early 1980s. In the 1990s some of the areas of highest unemployment are to be found in the London con-urbation.

The population 'in employment' figures seemed to show, in the 1970s, a trend which has now become quite common; the concept of the 'job ratio' rising, which is the employed population as a percentage of the residential population. This was a process which was clearly increasing in the 1950s. Even in those days certain cities such as Bristol, Derby, Portsmouth and Wolver-hampton were showing dramatic increases in the 'job ratio' with an increasing number of the working population commuting in and out of the city centres. It was this problem among others that the Barbican development (Fig. 2.4) in the City of London was originally designed to solve. The Barbican Committee realized that residential rents were unlikely to service the cost of the high value of sites in central London and therefore devised the concept of 'multi-land use' by putting flats on top of offices and shops and making the latter pay for the land, so that the land costs of the flats were nil. This was a theme strongly promoted by Bryan Anstey and others in the mid-1950s. The concept has recently re-emerged in the Government PPG 6 statement in 1996 concerning mixed-use inner city retail development. Unfortunately, the planning authorities at that time did not fully understand the concept of multi-land use and, forgetting that the City of London had until relatively recently been an area of multiple land use, stuck rigidly to the 'zoning' concept, a theme I will return to later.

The five main aims of the Barbican development, as described by the Corporation of the City of London, were:

Fig. 2.4. The Barbican in the City of London. An act of faith which created a new residential environment after the Second World War.

Firstly, and very simply, to rebuild the area in one concerted operation . . . secondly, to provide accommodation for all the major uses generally found in an urban area . . . thirdly, to secure a type of large scale development which can be successfully undertaken by private enterprise on a profitable basis . . . fourthly, to relieve the civic and public authorities of the burden of servicing the capital expenditure which has necessarily to be incurred in the compulsory purchase of the large area concerned. Fifthly, to provide a prototype for such a form of City development that will secure that concentration of human activities which gives power and effectiveness to Cities, whilst avoiding the congestion and confusion into which modern cities have fallen particularly with regard to their traffic problems.

The Corporation of London, according to the Barbican press release in 1970, investigated 'without success, the possibility of the private development of housing within the City' but it was not until 1959 that a detailed scheme was approved. By this time the Corporation had turned the Barbican into a cultural objective; to have people living in the City almost at any cost. The Barbican Centre has now become the home to the London Symphony Orchestra and the Royal Shakespeare Company, and also has an art gallery, conference facilities and the City University. Within the 40-acre site there are also schools, shops and recreational facilities plus on-site car parking. Although the original economic justification for the development got lost, from 1954 until the first tenants moved into apartments in 1968, there was a waiting list of residents. The Barbican today provides more than 2000 flats to accommodate more than 6000 residents, at a population density of 230 persons per acre.

Since the Barbican has been built, the strategic Guidance for London (1987) suggested an additional 200 dwellings be created in the City of London, a very modest target. However, generally towns and cities have not set housing targets to encourage private dwellings to move back into town centres. Chelsea Habour, a private up-market residential development by the P&O Group, is a rare example of such urban renewal. The London Docklands have also seen a significant quantity of private residential development. As I will discuss later, a few other cities have begun to see similar development.

Land use zoning

Over the years planning controls have done as much as anything to distort the housing market, despite the fact that the planning acts have largely aimed to improve the housing situation. If one considers the various planning controls which include the Town and Country Planning Act 1947, and its amendments in 1954, 1959, 1963 and onwards, plus the various rents acts, the controls on urban office development, the location of industry objectives, the tax relief on residential mortgages, etc., it is easy to see how the housing market has become influenced and distorted.

One of the influences relates to the concept of zoning. Zoning is an example of a planning instrument which has needed to be reshaped for some time. The zoning idea is summed up by Lewis Mumford: 'The City is essentially a place for diversified and mixed activities; yet in the case of industries like cementing chemical works, steel plants and slaughter houses, physical isolation is desirable and justifies relatively long journeys to work.'

Current zoning is determined by the Use Classes Order 1987 which amended the earlier 1972 Order. It divides land use into the following broad categories (of which there are many subclasses):

Class A – Retailing
Class B – Business, office, industrial, etc.
Class C – Residential, hotel, etc.
Class D – Non-residential, leisure. etc.

It is obvious that in certain circumstances zoning is necessary, both socially and economically. The question is whether zoning is justified in London or in any major cities, or even in towns where most of the employment is in the service sector. It is suggested that zoning has had the effect of raising land prices, encouraging urban sprawl and increasing unnecessary travel costs. As a result, large metropolitan areas are not necessarily a reflection of the consumer market's preference for spacious living, but to some extent reflect urban land use controls.

Long-distance commuting is expensive, not only in time and in terms of the private costs for the individual, but it is also socially expensive. Very few commuting transport systems anywhere in the world are self-financing; most commuter rail networks are subsidized by taxpayers. Twenty-five years ago the issue of home working was already being debated and the merits of commuting to office buildings in city centres questioned. At that time electronic facilities would have been far more expensive than today, but the issue of subsidising commuting was summed up by a company in San Francisco. They were asked why they did not connect their company to their office workers at home. They replied: 'But why should a company pay for such an expensive technological feat when the public will deliver the workers to the company free?' Since those days, the issues of public expenditure and reducing taxation have become more acute. The public purse is more reluctant than 25 years ago to subsidize travel. In a globally competitive world, reducing the need to commute expensive distances from place of residence to place of work becomes a financial necessity, not merely socially desirable. This concept lay behind the development of the Barbican in the immediate post-war decades; but what was an 'expensive technological feat' in the 1970s, is relatively inexpensive in the age of the Internet in the 1990s. This issue will be discussed in Chapter 3.

Mixed use development

The main theme discussed in *Reclaiming the City*, edited by Andy Coupland, is the concept of mixed use development. In 1996 the RICS also published *Mixed Use Development: Concept and Realities*, edited by Alan Rowley. The concept is that cities may be more sustainable if a policy of mixed use development is promoted reversing the trends towards strict land use zoning. As discussed in Chapter 1, the idea of sustainable development is complex. Andy Coupland has clearly set out the advantages and disadvantages of mixed land use, yet it is a clear truism; all towns and cities contain a mixture of land uses. However, over the last half century the forces of the market combined with zoning policies have created an increasing decentralization of residential, business employment and retail activity. If mixed use development is worth promoting, and if the forces of the market are to be encouraged in this direction, a far clearer idea of the problems associated with such land use is needed. As Alan Rowley observes, mixed use development is an ambiguous and multi-faceted concept.

Mixed uses within one building create both physical and legal problems. One example is the modular layout of a retail unit, in terms of the width of the unit and the necessity to avoid columns in Zone A (the window frontage) trading space. These retail design issues are often in conflict with possible uses above the unit. The modular width of office buildings, with the necessity to provide flexibility and the opportunity to subdivide an office floor, is often very different. It is this type of conflict of physical needs, with the market's aim to create economically efficient accommodation, which has been discussed over many years when mixed use developments have been suggested. Major schemes such as Spitalfields or Paternoster Square in the City of London, or far smaller schemes in town centres throughout the country, frequently come across this problem.

Linked to physical constraints are issues generated out of statutory regulations. The most obvious is the need for primary or secondary means of access to upper parts, particularly to comply with fire regulations. The conflict is amplified when a service yard area and/or car parking facilities are contemplated. In addition to physical constraints there are legal issues which frequently adversely affect the investment risk of projects. In *Reclaiming the City* Chris Marsh suggests that there is antipathy by investing institutions. There may be an element of truth in this statement but quantifying investment risk is the main constraint.

An example relates to residential dwellings over shops; most high streets in Great Britain contain vacant areas which were once dwellings over shop units. In addition to the physical constraints discussed above, investors have been wary of investing in residential investments in recent decades; successive statutes have protected residents at the expense of investment returns. The result, until the creation of Shorthold Residential Tenancies, was a steady reduction in private rented housing in Great Britain. In some areas of towns and cities there are now early signs of a reversal of this trend; private residential dwellings are returning to city centres. But other problems remain; should residents over shops have priority in terms of car parking or should car spaces be allocated to shoppers?

Residential renewal in London

Despite the example of the Barbican not being repeated, in the last decade there have been some indications that the process of counter-urbanization, with residents leaving London, has been reversed. As Geoff Marsh of the London Research Centre has discovered, the population of some of the inner Boroughs of London increased by more than 3% between 1981 and 1991 (Table 2.4), following many decades of decline, despite evidence that the population of Greater London may be falling still further.

Where did the population come from? Further analysis by Geoff Marsh identifies the sources of the migration into the London Boroughs. Of more than 77 000 people who moved into the Central London Boroughs in the decade to 1991, the majority, over 45 000, came from overseas. This is a reflection of the global nature of the urban problem; migration is both national and international. Towns and cities are competing on the world stage for residents! However, of more than 77 000 who came to London, more than 30 000 came from other areas of Great Britain, as can be seen in Table 2.5.

The London residential property market is one of the most well documented. The structural change in the market is illustrated by the changes in prices of housing between 1988 and 1995, as shown on Table 2.6. This was a period

Borough	1951	1981	1991
Camden	258	179	182
City	5	5	4
Hackney	265	185	188
Hammersmith and Fulham	241	151	156
Islington	271	166	174
Kensington and Chelsea	219	140	145
Lambeth	347	253	257
Southwark	338	218	227
Tower Hamlets	231	145	168
Wandsworth	331	262	265
Westminster	300	188	188
Total	2806	1892 (-32%)	1954 (+3.3%)

Table 2.4 London's resident population ('000s)

Source: London Research Centre, London 95, Table A1.

	Outer metropolitan area	Outer south-east	From rest of Britain	Overseas
Camden	775	636	1944	5993
City	44	33	77	127
Hackney	369	295	1062	2401
Hammersmith and Fulham	911	689	1928	4336
Islington	620	446	1409	2616
Kensington and Chelsea	676	619	1595	7811
Lambeth	776	710	2172	3753
Southwark	643	536	1501	2416
Tower Hamlets	534	361	1000	1669
Wandsworth	1527	1085	3069	4907
Westminster	1056	721	2332	9517
Total: 77 697, of which	7931	6131	18 089	45 546

Table 2.5 Migration to London Boroughs, Census 1991

Source: London Research Centre.

Post code	Postal district	Average price 1996	% Change since 1988
Top 10			
SE21	Dulwich	156 216	77.3
SW5	Earls Court	194 578	57.7
SW13	Barnes	236 644	56.3
W4	Chiswick	164 230	46.4
NW3	Hampstead	189 599	38.9
SW6	Fulham	173 551	38.4
W2	Paddington	192 383	36.2
SW10	West Brompton	187 848	35.5
W6	Hammersmith	152 764	34.5
W11	Notting Hill	195 849	32.6
Bottom 10			
E1	Stepney	93 493	-16.2
N17	Tottenham	57 128	-18.6
N9	Lower Edmonton	61 835	-18.7
E7	Forest Gate	55 202	-20.3
E15	Stratford	51 921	-22.7
E13	Plaistow	48 868	-23.8
N18	Hornsey	59 491	-24.3
SE2	Abbey Wood	51 688	-25.0
E6	East Ham	53 797	-25.4
E16	Victoria Docks	48 257	-32.4

Table 2.6 London residential property price changes: 1988 to 1996

Source: Halifax Building Society.

when Great Britain was in recession for much of the time, when mortgage repossessions reached an all-time high, and many other home owners struggled with negative equity – i.e. mortgages were often higher than the market value of their homes. Unemployment was also in the region of 10% or more for a number of years.

Although by the mid 1990s it was clear that there was a cyclical recovery in the economy of Great Britain, the structural change which had taken place since the 1980s, and the growth in income inequality discussed earlier, became illustrated by changing residential property prices; certain areas of London, such as Dulwich, Barnes and Hampstead, have continued to show very significant residential property price increases (see Table 2.6). Savills, international property consultants, have also noticed that prime Central London prices have increased faster than mainstream UK mortgaged property; in 1996 prices went up by 11.8% on average. At the other end of the scale certain postal districts in East London have done particularly badly; in Abbey Wood, East Ham and in the Victoria Docks, residential prices have fallen by 25% or more in this same time period.

With residential prices increasing so dramatically in certain parts of London and, according to the Richard Ellis survey of all office buildings over 1000 ft^2, with more than 15 million ft^2 of empty office buildings standing idle in the

Fig. 2.5. County Hall, London. The former home of the Greater London Council before redevelopment. The York Road buildings now contain more than 400 apartments.

capital in early 1996, it was not surprising that the entrepreneurial nature of the property market had found a partial solution. By mid-1995 Geoff Marsh at London Residential Research had identified more than 1000 residential units being created from buildings previously used as offices. Of these, the largest is the former office building of the Greater London Council, County Hall, York Road, Waterloo (Fig. 2.5); this building alone has sold more than 400 residential units.

Although no totally accurate figures are available, in the two years to mid-1996, more than 1 million ft^2 of former office buildings may have already been converted to residential use, as shown in Table 2.7.

In a further study for LPAC in mid-1996, Geoff Marsh estimated that over 100 office conversions involving 10 or more units had been completed, or had been in the planning system, in central and inner London since 1993, potentially creating some 3800 homes. Including small conversions, this rises to 4500 and the total redevelopment of some office buildings would add a further 1000 homes.

The question remains: are the natural forces of economic change sufficient to redress the problems clearly apparent in towns and cities across Great Britain? A list of office buildings converted into residential use (for example, Fig. 2.6) indicates that the private investment market will 'cherry pick' those buildings and those locations which are likely to appeal to the private residential market; other areas may continue to decline, and redundant office buildings will remain empty.

Address	Post code	Units created
Pattern House, 223/227 St John Street	EC1	20
Warner House, Warner Street	EC1	25
Cathedral Lodge, 115 Aldersgate Street	EC1	50
Red House, 49/53 Clerkenwell Road	EC1	20
44/49 Great Sutton Street	EC1	24
Herbal Hill Gardens	EC1	60
8 Northburgh	EC1	12
1/10 Summer Street	E1	25
34/39 East Smithfield	E1	41
38/44 Middlesex Street	E1	18
70/78 York Way	N1	20
Tyndale, Tyndale Terrace	N1	18
Gilbey House, JamestownRoad	NW1	76
Peninsula Heights, 93 Albert Embankment	SE1	36
Alaska, Phase One	SE1	50
Bankside Lofts, Hopton Street	SE1	129
County Hall, York Road	SE1	411
47/55 Gillingham Street	SW1	13
10/12 North Mews	WC1	14
Total		1,062

Table 2.7 Office to residential conversions

Source: London Residential Research, mid-1995

Fig. 2.6. 9 Hill Street, West End of London. The inside of a renovated town house, converted to commercial use in wartime. When temporary planning use expired it was converted back to residential use in the 1980s. (Photograph: Damond Lock Grabowski & Partners.)

The age of the population

Linked to this issue is the problem of the 'demographic time bomb'. Internationally and nationally the population of the mature countries is ageing. The problem of an ageing population is even greater in Germany and Japan than in the UK or USA. Countries like Malaysia are also experiencing an ageing population, but there is a lag of more than 30 years. The international problem is summarized in Table 2.8 for the period 1990–2050, and the ageing population in the UK is given in greater detail in Table 2.9.

Table 2.8 Percentage of population over 60 years old: an international comparison

	1990	2020	2050
USA	16.6	19.2	28.9
UK	20.8	23.0	29.5
Germany	20.3	26.5	32.5
Japan	17.3	29.0	34.4
Malaysia	5.7	8.0	22.1

Source: United Nations.

	% 65–79	% 80+
1971	11.0	2.0
1981	12.0	3.0
1991	12.0	4.0
1994	12.0	4.0
2001	11.0	4.0
2011	12.0	5.0
2021	14.0	5.0
2031	16.0	7.0

Table 2.9 Demographic change in Great Britain: proportion of pension age UK population

Source: Office for National Statistics.

With an ageing population, and more single person households, it is not surprising that the average household size in terms of the number of occupants continues to fall and that there has been a significant growth in the number of old people's care homes (Table 2.10). By 1995 the top 16 public companies providing long-term care for the elderly were already providing more than 25 000 beds, but the number of 'for profit' nursing home places in Great Britain had soared from 52 000 in 1987 to 178 800 by 1994. This is perhaps a partial solution to the urban residential problem; there could be positive discrimination towards care homes for the elderly in inner city areas. In terms of building and design there are a wide range of possibilities, including quiet courtyard/landscaped secure clusters of care homes able to enjoy the economic benefits of scale, yet close to established town centre facilities. However, few physical town centre plans have identified this as a preferred land use.

Recent ideas

The concept of development for residential communities within city centres is producing some disparate, and at times fairly unrealistic, thinking. The following illustrates some of the issues which have been identified.

In 1995 the Disney Corporation hosted a gathering in Paris to address *The City in 2020*. Leading participants from industries across the world, including architects and sociologists, debated and discussed for several days and illustrated a number of ideas:

Changing work practices, technology and transport patterns will fundamentally alter the communities we live in over the next twenty five years. . . . villages, towns and cities and the strength of the human attachment, and identification with place, would counter some of the more pessimistic theories and predictions of the decline of communities. . . . the home of 2020 would be a major contributor to life style quality. It would be smarter, self maintained and would contain more electronics. It would combine the real environment with the virtual world, perhaps creating an increased demand for historic environments, or some actual link with the past. . . . the eternal search for quality of life would go on – but in twenty-five years, greater choice would make the quest as difficult as ever.

	No. of homes	No. of beds
ANS	36	2 206
Apta Nursing Services	33	1 294
Ashbourne	46	3 444
BUPA	30	1 267
Care UK	20	973
Community Hospital	15	823
Craegmoor	43	2 011
Cresta Care	56	3 310
Exceler	43	2 123
Extendicare	14	1 018
Goldsborough	32	1 546
Highfield Group	25	1 401
Lifestyle Care	21	1 060
Quality Care	40	2 046
St Andrews	38	1 927
Sandown	31	1 414
Speciality Care*	28	1 488
TC Group	130	12 042
Tamaris*	27	1 490
West. Health Care	100	6 352

Table 2.10 Number of homes and beds operated by major care home quoted companies and selected companies with over 1000 beds at 18 November 1996

Note: six homes (356 beds) currently included under Speciality Care have been sold to Tamaris. The deal has been signed but is awaiting completion.
Source: Laing & Buisson Publications Limited.

In addition to this major Disney Corporation international conference, there are an on-going series of events and other conferences looking at the future of cities under the general banner of 'urban management and strategy'. However many of these are unfocused in terms of developing business strategies for towns and cities. For instance, in the 1995 Reith Lectures, Sir Richard Rogers addressed some of the issues concerning the future of the cities, particularly London. Once again he addressed the problem, without suggesting how the forces of the private market could be harnessed to create cultured, self-sustainable cities. An example of this dilemma is as follows. As a way to reduce pollution and congestion, he suggested:

> One way would be partially to finance public transport by a metropolitan tax levied on residents and employers . . . travelling by car would begin to be perceived as a luxury.

Here is a recipe for increasing the problem; you do not solve city centre problems by taxing those who work and live in city centres more than those who live outside the cities. Such a policy is liable to increase urban costs and to accelerate the process of outward migration and polarization of wealth within the city for those who remain. This problem has arisen in a number of cities in the United States of America where similar taxation issues have been raised. The only partial success relates to the USA concept of BIDS (Business

Improved Districts), a business association concept at a micro level aiming to tidy up inner urban business areas. However, the future of towns and cities must not be perceived as a local problem; it is increasingly a national and international issue.

The New Labour approach on the surface appears to offer some solution. In the 1996 document *Reinventing the City*, Keith Vaz says: 'Britain's cities have been neglected for far too long. They need to be supported to enable them to compete with the best in Europe and the best in the world.' However the document comes up with very few hard ideas to achieve this laudable objective.

Some of the inner city legislation so far . . .

The issue of tackling inner cities as areas of waste land, empty buildings, high dereliction, high unemployment and an unbalanced population structure, combined with low morale, were first formally addressed by a Labour government in *Policies for the Inner Cities*, a White Paper published in 1977 by Peter Shore, the then Secretary of State for the Environment. It suggested that there should be greater resources and a priority for inner cities areas, a co-ordinated approach by central and local government working together, and measures to help strengthen inner area economies to encourage employment. These objectives later appeared in the Inner Urban Area Act 1978 which gave specific powers to selected inner city local authorities.

As we now know, this initial attempt more than 20 years ago to tackle inner city problems was followed in the 1980s with such ideas as Urban Development Corporations, Enterprise Zones, the Scottish Enterprise (including former Scottish Development Agency), the Welsh Development Agency plus the Land Authority for Wales, Derelict Land Grant, City Grant, City Challenge and many more. The issue of contaminated land and the Environment Agency set up following the Environment Act 1995 further complicates the situation. Contamination inhibits urban renewal. Many of these objectives were then taken on by English Partnerships, which was formerly launched on 1 April 1994. It describes its role as follows:

> As a government sponsored agency, our role is to bring together the private, public and voluntary sectors to create economic growth, employment opportunities and environmental improvements in areas of need throughout England. In partnership with others, the developments will be focused on industrial, commercial, residential and leisure uses, together with land made safe or brought back into use for green or recreational purposes. Through the reclamation and re-use of vacant, contaminated or derelict land and buildings, our programmes will be geared to improving the image, quality of life and economic opportunities for inner city and urban and rural communities. By adopting a strategic approach, combine it with an operational network of regional offices, we aim to ensure that the projects we support will make a lasting contribution to economic and environmental regeneration.

English Partnerships completed its first full year on 31 March 1995. In the foreword to the annual report, Lord Walker stated: 'Our priority, therefore, is to support projects that create long-term employment opportunities, particularly in manufacturing industries, as a key to successful economic regeneration.' Herein lies a dilemma; the overall objectives of English Partnerships, and their sister bodies the Welsh Development Agency and Scottish Enterprise, deserve support and encouragement from all those concerned with the future of towns and cities. However, it is far from clear how, on its own, English Partnerships can redress the growing social imbalance in urban areas which has been accelerated by greater global competition, partly resulting from international financial deregulation, corporate restructuring and the impact of information technology.

The challenge for all central urban areas, including apparently prosperous towns in the Green Belt around London, is to attract middle-income housing (with or without families) back into the city centres. Here is the Achilles' heel of the issue; if those concerned with urban problems at a national and local level can address this one simple problem, retailing will return to city centres, jobs will return to city centres, social problems associated with the clustering of 'underclass' citizens within inner urban areas will diminish and city centres will once again be perceived as safe and desirable. A simple business strategy for all inner towns and cities should be to increase the number of middle-income residents; this is a finite target which can be monitored from year to year, and can be measured from one decade to the next. If clearly stated as an urban objective, it would not be regarded as gerrymandering – the process of influencing the residential voting population. But if this simple objective is to be adopted, it will only be successful if the total physical and social infra-structure of town and city centres is improved, especially the provision of improved education (discussed earlier in this chapter) and health facilities, to attract middle-income families.

In June 1996 the Department of the Environment issued a revised *Planning Policy Guidance Note 6* concerned with 'Town Centres and Retail Develop-ments'. This note stated:

> The key features of this guidance are:
> i.   On planning for town centres and retailing:
>   – emphasis on plan led approach to promoting development into town centres . . .
> ii. On town centres:
>   – promotion of mixed used development and retention of key town centre uses: . . .

Section 2.1.3 dated:

> . . . a mixture of small businesses, houses or offices in or near town centres and the occupation of flats above shops, can increase activity and therefore personal safety while ensuring that buildings are kept in good repair. Residents and workers stimulate shopping, restaurants and cáfes, and other businesses to serve them, and so in turn add to vitality.

Here at last is an admission that residential development may have a place in town centres, but there is no clear guidance on setting clear residential development goals. What sort of residential use should be encouraged? What about car access and parking? What about improved education facilities? Section 2.1.8 of the guidance note states:

> . . . although retailing should continue to underpin such centres, it is only part of what ensures the health of town centres.

The overall tone of the *Planning Policy Guidance Note 6* suggests that intensive retailing in town centres represents a status quo, which should be maintained regardless of the environment and travel/congestion consequence, and without paying attention to the trends which I have identified in the decline of commercial activity generally in town centre areas. This theme has echoes in the consultative paper: *Planning Policy Guidance Note 1*, issued in July 1996. It states:

> A key role of the planning system is to enable the provision of homes and public buildings, investment and jobs in a way which is consistent with the principles of sustainable development.

But what do town planners think?

In connection with the subject of sustainable development, in 1996 I wrote to a number of planning officers across Great Britain, in city centres and in smaller towns, and asked them:

1. What is your current planning policy towards residential development in your town centre?
2. With reference to 1. above, what is your strategy for encouraging middle-income household developments (with or without children) within your town centre?
3. With specific reference to residential development, what is your current (and future) attitude towards car parking and road access in the town centre?

This request for information produced a mixture of responses, some of which followed on from the theme of the *Planning Policy Guidance Note 6*. For instance, the reply from one town in the south of England stated:

> Town centre housing is seen as a means of helping create 24-hour communities and provide a range of housing types and reduce the need to commute, relieve traffic congestion and encourage the use of public transport.

However, the same reply went on to say:

> As you may know, planning authorities cannot prescribe the income levels of occupants of residential accommodation; however, bearing in mind that the town's greatest need is for family housing, and that there is a substantial need for affordable family housing (particularly homes for

rent) this type of accommodation is encouraged wherever possible subject to the availability of the site and its location including availability of amenity space and parking.

The council concerned stated that they were working with a number of Housing Associations to provide low-cost affordable housing. However, the council concerned did not acknowledge that such a policy would encourage the polarization of housing type, with the town centre continuing to harbour low-income housing, without encouraging a more balanced type of residential development.

Another council replied as follows:

> In practice most housing will be for middle-income households because households on lower incomes cannot afford market house prices and rents, and high-income households will probably choose to live outside the town centre in lower density areas.

Herein lies a total confusion. The town's planning officer's opinion did not match reality; the town concerned had very little middle-income housing in its centre, but did contain a number of empty, semi-derelict, buildings.

Another town council in the Midlands wrote:

> Significant progress has been made in recent years in achieving more residential units, and these have generally been Housing Association accommodation often with relatively low rents targeted at mainly single people.

Here again is a town centre encouraging low-income dwellings in its city centre rather than redressing the social housing imbalance.

Another city in the north of England stated its objective was to increase the number of people living in the city centre but that:

> Residential development in the city centre would be supported only where both future residents and existing uses and users of buildings are able to coexist and function efficiently and effectively.

This particular city recognized the opportunity to bring young people back into the city as a way of creating life and vitality but also recognized:

> The creation of student 'ghettos' or large-scale residential schemes, which are poorly related to the established patterns of city life and activities, would conflict with the spirit of the city centre living policy, which promotes a more flexible and holistic approach to city planning.

Here is the essence of a more balanced approach to residential development, but the reality is that many cities simply do not have a policy to encourage middle-income housing back into the city centre as a way of recreating a balanced residential population.

Another northern city, rather than addressing this issue, referred to the problem by stating (these are the exact words):

A balance has to be struck between residential amenity and the special nature of the city centre; as such it is likely that outwith the existing established residential areas, the type of environment will only be suitable for certain types of residents and not, for example, families with young children.

Rather than recognize the problem and develop a strategy to encourage middle-income families back into the city centre (requiring improved education facilities), the city appears to be allowing the current zoning principle to be perpetuated, perhaps without recognizing the detrimental effect this is likely to continue to have over the longer term.

One of the more interesting replies I received came from a town centre in the middle of Great Britain which had been interested in obtaining finance from central government sources. As a result of its endeavours it had commissioned an audit of its town centre and began to put together a new business strategy. Within this new strategy, the concept of an 'Urban Village' was being developed. The documentation relating to this particular town centre said:

> In the absence of a single land ownership it is vital for the local authority to play an active role in bringing sites forward for development and to find mechanisms to promote appropriate development and to ensure that benefits are shared.

It went on to explain:

> The aim is to repopulate the centre with a balanced community mix and land uses, designed to be compatible and complementary in the form of an 'Urban Village', recapturing many of the traditional urban living qualities.

However, this city centre, in common with many in the economically developed world, faces the major problem of finance. It suggested:

> This decision-making role could involve the raising of a 'local levy' or charge to finance improvements to the town centre, usually purchasing additional services through the local authority.

Here, yet again, lies the problem; by charging a city centre a levy, there is a tendency to make the city centre even less desirable than edge-of-city or out-of-town locations. Unless this issue is faced at a national level, such a programme of levies is unlikely to assist the concept of an urban village.

Integral to all these issues is car parking for residential developments. In a car-owning market economy, the ability to use one's car is extremely influencial for many. While some town and city centres come up with statements such as: 'In many cases, it is neither possible nor appropriate to have car parking, particularly in the city centre core area' or 'The provision of convenient, secure high-quality car parking with an appropriate charging policy which supports the vitality and viability of the centre is essential', other town centres find themselves in a dilemma. For instance, one council in the south of England stated:

The Council has a more relaxed policy on car parking for residential development in the town centre, i.e. less car parking is required. Access by road to town centre residential developments will be indirectly improved by the continuing introduction of a park and ride system for non-residential uses of the town centre.

A signpost to the future

Here at last is a move in the right direction, but middle-income families (with or without children) are unlikely to move into town and city centres unless there is adequate car-parking provision. This is not to say that the use of the car should be encouraged, but town planners have to face up to reality; we live in a car-dominated society. Unless city centres are prepared to provide more than sufficient car spaces for town centre residents, very little city centre residential development for middle-income housing is likely to be created. Such a policy of creating private residential car spaces should be pursued as complementary to an active policy of encouraging the use of public transport, together with road calming measures, to discourage through traffic.

In recent years there have been some examples of in-town development, and the Chancellor of the Exchequer's stated objective in 1995, to allow Housing Investment Trusts to be listed on the London Stock Exchange, is part of this strategy. This follows on from the concept of the Business Expansion Scheme, a tax-efficient vehicle created by government in the 1980s to encourage investment. The suggestion is that Housing Investment Trusts should form part of the government's continuing attempt to expand the private rented sector, which is slightly ironic after many decades of encouraging a home-owning democracy.

To qualify for an immediate Stock Exchange listing, it was suggested that 75% of the gross assets of the property investment trust would be in building rather than cash. However, the government initially decreed that the value of housing in such portfolios should be limited to £85 000 per property outside London and £125 000 in London. This is unlikely to encourage a substantial development of city centre middle-income housing which, at 1995/6 prices, is often worth more than £85 000. However, firms such as Bradford Property Trust have shown that large residential rental companies can survive.

Despite problems, there are already a few examples of middle-income housing being created in city centres, although not necessarily using the Housing Investment Trust route. The few flagship examples include private housing development around St Paul's Square in the Old Jewellery Quarter and in the Broad Street area of Birmingham, on South Shields Riverside in Tyne and Wear, in Hulme on the south side of Manchester (with significant government assistance, Fig. 2.7) and at the Canal Wharf in Leeds. The opening in 1996 of the Bordesley, public–private, £65 million 1000 unit housing scheme in Birmingham (Fig. 2.8), shows that the creation of a new mixed urban village is possible. The Friern Park, Barnet in north London is another mixed use scheme, including housing as well as retail development, being created within an urban area.

In Brindleyplace, in the centre of Birmingham (Fig. 2.9), a run-down area of factories and workshops has given way to a mixture of offices, restaurants,

Fig. 2.7. New housing in Hulme, Manchester. A City Challenge project bringing urban regeneration, creating a sense of place where cars are adequately catered for without encouraging their use. (Photograph: Hulme Regeneration Limited.)

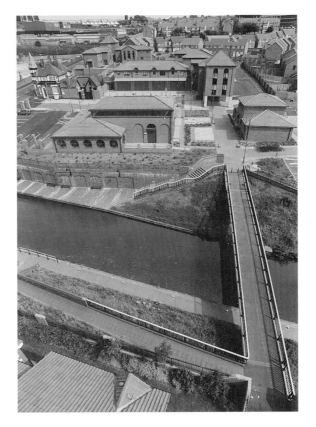

Fig. 2.8. Bordesley Residential Development created by Birmingham Heartlands Development Corporation, involving a new mixed urban village containing 1000 housing units. (Photograph: Birmingham Heartlands Development Corporation.)

Fig. 2.9. Symphony Court, Brindleyplace, Birmingham, awarded The Silver Award by What House *magazine for the Best Urban Renewal Project. (Photograph: Crosby Homes (Midlands) Limited.)*

shops and residential developments. Symphony Court contains 143 houses and apartments, despite the fact that apartment prices ranged from £72 500 for one-bedroom flats and up to £275 000 for three-bedroom penthouse dwellings. The dilemma is that, to make the Symphony Court development successful, it has had to be designed on the 'fortress principle' with measures taken to discourage young drinking groups. Symphony Court has been developed as a private, secure compound, shut off from the general public. As *The Daily Telegraph* pointed out on 5 June 1996, 'but that's the price of persuading the middle classes to move back into the city'.

Although all these schemes, demonstrating residential development in inner urban areas, are to be welcomed as creating urban renewal, a radical shift in urban development thinking is urgently required in a country with a population of more than 50 million and with an estimated 4.4 million extra homes needed in the next 20 years.

CHAPTER 3
Technology: the catalyst for urban change

Two overriding considerations dominate the development of urban areas: the gregarious nature of mankind as an animal species, and man's ability to use technology in an innovative way. In the late twentieth century the advent of information technology both intrigues and frightens us in equal measure. How will urban areas change?

The city of the dead antedates the city of the living, according to Lewis Mumford in his book *The City In History*. He goes on to say:

> . . . Original aspects of temporary settlement have to do with sacred things, not just with physical survival; they relate to a more valuable and meaningful kind of life, with a consciousness that entertains past and future. . . . Thus, even before the city as a place of fixed residence, it begins as a meeting place to which people periodically return; the magnet comes from the container and its ability to attract non-residents. The first germ of the city, then, is the ceremonial meeting place that serves as the goal for pilgrimage; a site to which family or clan groups are drawn back, at seasonable intervals, because it concentrates, in addition to any natural advantages it may have, certain 'spiritual' or supernatural powers, powers of higher potency and greater duration, of wider cosmic significance than the ordinary processes of life.

It has been mankind's ability to mix these spiritual needs with the advance of technology which has created the urban structures we know today. Asa Briggs, in his book *Victorian Cities*, says that the Victorian cities:

> are the cities of the railway and tramway age, of the age of steam and of gas, of a society sometimes restless. . . . Perhaps their outstanding feature was hidden from public view – their hidden network of pipes and drains

and sewers, one of the biggest technical and social achievements of the age, a sanitary 'system' more comprehensive than the transport system.

Technical achievements are at the heart of all urban change. So, what is technology? According to *The Penguin Dictionary of Economics*, technology is the:

Sum of knowledge of the means and methods of producing goods and services. Technology is not merely applied science, because it often runs ahead of science – things are often done without precise knowledge of who or why they are done except they are effective.

The application of technology is an integral part of the development of towns and cities, in the past, in the present and for the future. The technology of creating heat and light in buildings, for instance, has changed dramatically in less than 50 years with the advent of gas-fired central heating, air-conditioning systems and cheap electrical lighting. The impact of technology, for good or bad, will always be with us. The history of the impact of technology on urban areas is that, as the technology develops, it has an accelerating impact on urban development. It is the impact of technology which economists have failed to measure and understand, and physical town planners (urban land managers) have not anticipated; unless we begin to understand its significance, technology will continue to rule urban areas, rather than be harnessed to benefit our towns and cities. One thing is certain: the advance of technology is relentless. In the following pages I have considered some of the more important uses of technology which have shaped, and continued to shape, our urban environment.

Construction material technology

Although technology influences our lives in numerous ways, the most obvious long-lasting application of technology to urban development is that of construction material. The remnants of the ancient world are represented in the stone structures we see today, ranging from the Parthenon in Athens, the Pyramids in Egypt or Stonehenge in Britain. Each of these examples is interestingly a place of worship, bearing out the thesis promoted by Lewis Mumford.

The overall layout of towns and cities, using stone (as well as other materials), has not changed dramatically in many thousands of years. Visitors to Pompeii or Herculaneum on the western coast of Italy, or to Corinth on the north edge of the Peloponnese in Greece, are sometimes surprised to see how similar the layouts of these ancient towns were, compared with the patterns of modern urban cities. The agora (marketplace) and the streets leading from the agora are repeated in towns and cities in central business districts or in shopping malls across the world in the twentieth century. However, it was the advanced use of iron as a construction material which has changed certain aspects of cities. With the advent of the Industrial Revolution, the combination of iron and coal (as a source of energy) enabled mankind to develop iron and steel structures not possible in the ancient world. These range from the Eiffel Tower in Paris to the construction of bridges, the railway network and factory development. The construction of the first iron bridge by a Quaker, Abraham Darby in 1777 (shown in Fig. 3.1), led this new form of construction.

It was the application of coal and steel technology which enabled urban development to accelerate in Great Britain in the nineteenth century: such development in Germany, or even France, had to wait until the late nineteenth and early twentieth century to become industrialized. Urban areas grew both at the source of the primary material, the coal and iron ore, and in the industrialized cities such as Birmingham, Manchester and Glasgow. The legacy of that development remains today.

Cement, as a building material, was pioneered by the Romans. The Pantheon of Ancient Rome bears witness to being the first cement structure. In the twentieth century it has been the advanced use of concrete (a mixture of cement and aggregate) which has created a new ability for mankind to develop urban structures, ranging from roads and bridges, to shops, factories, offices and housing. Prefabrication (for example, the estate shown in Fig. 3.2), and the adaptation of system building, further accelerated the use of concrete as a building material. Combined with the enduring qualities of brick and tile, concrete has transformed many built environments and de-humanized others.

Fig. 3.1. Iron technology. Ironbridge, Shropshire, built in 1777 by Abraham Darby. An early use of iron in urban construction. (Photograph: Ironbridge Gorge Museum Trust.)

Neither town planners nor economists anticipated the advent of the uses of concrete and system building; it was left to the architects to prescribe this innovative material (see, for example, the concrete paving in Fig. 3.3). Le Corbusier was the twentieth-century architect who has had most influence applying the concept of concrete structures and became the visionary who influenced concrete urban developments more than most. His book *The Radiant City* provided a blueprint for urban development and was copied throughout the world from Roehampton to Rotterdam, from Algiers to Antwerp, from Paris to Prague, from Manchester to Moscow and many cities beyond. Brasilia, the purpose-built capital of Brazil, is just one example (of which there are many) where the architectural concepts of Le Corbusier were combined with the technology of concrete, to create a new urban environment.

Yet the application of this technology has not always been regarded as a success. President Havel, when being shown residential concrete town blocks on the edge of Prague, is reported as saying 'but rabbit hutches are for rabbits'. In St Louis USA, Birkenhead UK and in other cities, dynamite has removed the misused applications of concrete technology. Let us hope that the future application of concrete will be as inspiring as that of Pier Luigi Nervi for the 1960 Rome Olympic Games.

Recent applications of concrete have included the factory prefabrication of toilet pods for prisons and student accommodation, subsequently imported ready made from Scandinavia.

Farm technology

The advancement of material technology has moved simultaneously with that of bio-technology and agro-technology. The Agricultural Revolution of the later eighteenth and early nineteenth century in Britain was partly linked to the better use of crops, as well as the process of turning open land into 'enclosures' and crop rotation which improved agricultural production. Without improvements in bio-technology, and improvements in the productivity of farm land, cities would not have developed, as there would have been insufficient food to feed the urban population. One has only to look at the location of cities in the ancient world to realize that it was the productive capabilities of the agricultural hinterland which enabled certain cities to grow. Over the centuries the development of different forms of grain, fruit and, more recently, potatoes and animals have enabled food production to exceed the immediate local demand and to export food to cities.

In recent decades the bio-tech revolution has been linked to genetic engineering and plant breeding generally, advancing the ability of plants to produce abnormally high yields. Genetic engineering, or its earlier version known as genetic selection, also enabled animal breeding to develop and improve the productivity of livestock production generally. With the arrival of BSE and other problems there are worries that the bio-tech revolution may need more control. However, it was the advances made in mechanical technology which have allowed bio-technology to make its greatest advances. During the course of the twentieth century corn production has evolved from steam-powered threshing machines to reaper binder harvesters and, during the last 50 years, self-propelled combine harvesters associated with mechanical straw

Fig. 3.2. Concrete technology. The Roehampton Estate, South West London, used prefabricated concrete material.

Fig. 3.3. Corporate concrete technology. Concrete paving in Lower Broughton, Salford, Manchester.

Fig. 3.4. Water technology. Quarry Bank Mill, Cheshire. Originally built in the eighteenth century, powered by a water wheel. The first steam engine was built in 1810. (Photograph: Quarry Bank Mill Trust Limited.)

Fig. 3.5. Water technology. The River Wey in Surrey. Water transport dominated urban development in the early nineteenth century.

balers. This dramatic improvement in productivity, caused by mechanization, is just one example to illustrate how agro-technology has enabled city populations to expand.

The mechanization of farming is also illustrated by the harvesting of cotton. It is estimated that in 1949 only 6% of the cotton in the southern states of American was harvested mechanically, by 1964 78% was harvested using mechanical means, but by 1972 100% of all cotton picked was extracted from plants using machines.

Not only has mechanization, and the advancement of technology generally, dramatically increased the productive capabilities of farmland to feed urban areas, it has also released labour from rural areas, causing a migration to towns and cities of the developed economies of the world in both the nineteenth and twentieth centuries. In the late twentieth century this is also taking place with alarming speed in the so-called 'developing world'. The urbanization of Asian countries, including mainland China, is accelerating.

Water technology

Water technology is another form of technology which goes to the heart of the development of all cities, both past and present. One can clearly see the development of industrialized urban areas in the late eighteenth century as depending upon water power. The Quarry Bank Mill, on the south side of Manchester, is a living example of a weaving mill, still in working order, and originally based upon water power (Fig. 3.4). However, water has also provided the means of transport between cities. Until the seventeenth century the role of the sea was an important factor determining the growth of many cities including Athens, Venice, London and Oslo. But it was the development of canal systems, with their associated tow paths in the early years, which advanced many inland urban areas. From Berlin to Birmingham, cities developed an inland system that was based on a network of water transport routes. At the same time, major cities developed by linking both sea travel with inland water travel. Cities as far apart as Paris, Manchester and Chicago benefited from the use of mechanized water transport during the late nineteenth and early twentieth century.

Today, many of these inland water routes are little used for freight or human transport, yet it is only recently that urban planners have appreciated their opportunities for tourism and reinvigorating decaying urban areas. In Birmingham, Leeds and even smaller towns such as Guildford, there is far greater emphasis placed upon urban development facing on to existing waterways, predominantly used for leisure purposes in the late twentieth century (Fig. 3.5).

Steam technology

Steam technology, and the resulting railway technology, has had a major impact on urban development since the 1820s (Fig. 3.6). In 1804 Richard Trevithick had not only developed a steam engine, but had also created a locomotive driven by steam. It can be said that the 'age of steam' started when the Trevithick 'steamer on wheels' appeared. The railway passenger system began effectively in 1825 when George Stevenson's 'Rocket' pulled passenger-filled carriages at four and half miles per hour between Liverpool and Manchester. Parliament had sanctioned the first public railway in 1801, with the Surrey Iron Railway between Wandsworth and Croydon. Although there was only 1857 miles of track in 1842, by 1910, at the peak of the 'railway age' 23 387 miles of track covered Great Britain, as shown in Table 3.1. During this period Parliament authorized the construction of numerous lines and the 'Railway Kings' became a powerful influence on members of Parliament, perhaps equivalent to the road haulage lobby in recent decades. In 1845 the Land

Fig. 3.6. Steam technology. From 1820 onwards, the steam railway system increasingly influenced urban development. Urban electric railway technology is in the same picture.

Fig. 3.7. Urban railway technology. Edgware Road London Underground Station, upgraded to meet the functional use of the station with cultural nostalgia concerns to retain original materials. (Photograph: Format 2/Damond Lock Grabowski & Partners.)

Fig. 3.8. Urban railway technology. The new Greater Manchester Metro, first opened in 1992.

Fig. 3.9. Railway technology. Eastham Rake railway station on Merseyside, recently opened having been constructed with grant aid from the European Union.

Year	Miles
1842	1 857
1854	8 954
1870	15 537
1900	20 073
1910	23 387
1963	17 500
1967	13 000

Table 3.1 Rail lines open in Great Britain

Source: G.I. Savage, *An Economic History of Transport.*

Clauses Consolidation Act regularized the procedure for land purchase by public undertakings, including railway companies. In the same year the Railway Clauses Consolidation Act was passed prescribing a standard form for the enormous volume of railway bills. As the monopoly power of the railways increased, so did state involvement. Various Railway and Canal Traffic Acts were passed relating to such matters as the system of freight charges and the duty of companies to the public. It was estimated in 1930 that, in the previous 100 years, there had been 200 Acts of Parliament relating to railways. State involvement in the railway technology of Great Britain has existed as long as the railways have been in existence, yet few urban planners have fully anticipated its impact on urban development.

In the past there have been a few co-ordinated attempts to relate land use to the growth or decline of railways. Railways, however, played a significant part in urban development from their early days. Perhaps one of the best examples in the twentieth century was the Metropolitan Railway Company which, in the pre-1939 era, bought, leased and sold property adjacent to its stations, including the air rights over its tracks. Out in the countryside, at places such as Wembley Park and Harrow on the Hill, the residential development became known as 'Metro Land', while at the town end of the tracks, the development of high-class flats occurred, as for example over Baker Street station. In 1887, when the Underground railway had reached Golders Green, land values increased by 600%, and when the line was extended in 1923 the population of Hendon and Edgware increased from 59 000 to 162 000.

In *Garden Cities of Tomorrow* Ebenezer Howard envisaged a garden city relying on comprehensive railway systems for internal communications. Le Corbusier's ideas for a linear city in the 1920s were also founded essentially on a sound transport strategy, including public transport. The suburbs which grew between 1850 and 1920 owe their existence primarily to the railways, and their development during this period, before the imposition of statutory town planning 'controls'. The population distributed itself away from the crowded city centres and within easy walking distance of railway stations.

The first suburbs were really the product of the railway age. As Lewis Mumford observed, as soon as the motor car appeared, the human scale of suburbs changed and residential areas spread out in an amorphous and low-density mass as semi-detached suburbia expanded. In spite of the motor car age there are still some towns, particularly within the Green Belt around London, where suburban sprawl has not been significant and a 'human scale' relationship still exists between residential accommodation and residential land use. The railways also altered the nature of land use in city centres. Working-class housing and a fever hospital were originally on the sites of what is now known as St Pancreas and King's Cross Station. At these and most other terminal stations, both in London and elsewhere, hotels were built. This is yet another example of the way in which various railway companies tried to co-ordinated their transport facilities with urban land use.

Not only has the state always been a dominant factor in the development of the railway systems, so too have financial issues been associated with the industry – a fact which is unlikely to diminish even with privatization. The financial issues, both in a positive and negative way, have in turn influenced land use patterns associated with rail transport, particularly in urban areas. In the early days of railway construction in the nineteenth century, net receipts as a percentage of total paid-up capital had been 6–10%. This percentage slowly fell to around 4% by 1860 and then to 3.5% by 1912. Apart from the very early days, investment in railways in Great Britain has never been very profitable, as judged from a strictly financial point of view, yet urban land use has depended on this form of technology.

The Railway Act of 1921 led to the formation of the big four railway companies from the numerous small companies in an attempt to make railways more profitable. Although £51 million was anticipated as the annual revenue from these four companies, by 1928 only £41 million was received annually. This fell further to less than £29 million by 1938. It was in 1930, during the recession of revenue from passengers and other traffic, that the late president of the London, Midland and Scottish group, Lord Stamp, initiated a committee to examine sites and buildings which might contain elements for productive development. As a result, for example, when Wembley Central was rebuilt in 1932, it included a row of revenue earning shops. In reality very few sites were developed in this way.

By the Acts of Parliament in 1923 and 1933, the Great Western Railway Company, originally developed by Isambard Kingdom Brunel, was authorized to erect housing, shops and other buildings for let. Considerable advantages of these powers were taken by this railway company. Two examples of the development by this company during the period were the blocks of shops, flats and maisonettes developed in West Acton and at Oxford Road, Tilehurst. On the nationalization of the railways these powers, formerly held by the Great Western Railway Company, were withdrawn by the Transport Act of 1947, except where development was incorporated within a structure required primarily for railway purposes, such as shops within a station.

In the same way that the growth of railway technology had a considerable influence on urban development, the decline also had an impact. Following the nationalization of the railway system on 1 January 1948, there was a further attempt to make the railway pay. Yet again there was a lack of government guidance on pricing, very little control on investment of capital, practically no co-ordination with other nationalized industries at that time and no co-ordination with urban land use. The largest problem was costing and accounting for the railway's activities. The 1953 Transport Act was an attempt to give the railway greater freedom in disguising what its charges should be. However, it was not until 1961 that a government paper *The Financial and Economic Objectives of the Nationalized Industries* (Cmnd 1337) set out rules and guidelines to budget the performance of nationalized industries; it suggested that 'socially justifiable' services were to be separately identified. The railway was given a better start when the Transport Act of 1962 gave power to a new British railways board. The aim was to follow the objectives of the white paper, and to this end Dr Beeching produced his famous report *The Reshaping of British Railways* in 1963. This was surprisingly the first detailed study of the British railway system and it identified a number of problems. For instance, it was found that one-third of the then 17 500 miles carried only 1% of passengers, and understandably did not cover its cost. Even on high-density routes money was being lost due to peak flow demands. Outside peak hours the railway assets remained idle. The aim of the report was to make the railway system self-financing and eliminate the deficits by 1970. As a result, over 4000 miles of track were closed by 1967, while the surplus land was sold to raise capital for new investments.

Urban railway technology

From the 1920s onwards urban tram systems also declined. The larger cities finally withdrew their trams: 1949 (Manchester), 1950 (Cardiff and Newcastle), 1952 (London), 1953 (Birmingham), 1954 (Belfast), 1956 (Edinburgh), 1957 (Liverpool), 1959 (Leeds), 1960 (Leeds) and 1962 (Glasgow).

The decline of railway and tram technology was as influential on urban developments as its earlier growth; its decline increased the dependence on road-based transport technology. However, one of the lasting impacts of the railway system was the urban rail network. By the early twentieth century there was a growth in size and importance of a suburban electric rail network around London (Fig. 3.7). The growth of these locomotives during the 1950s, and the more recent innovation of diesel turbo-electric locomotives, has continued to provide a means of transport in urban areas.

Despite the privatization of the rail network in 1995/96, railway technology will continue to have an important effect on future urban land use. Privatization may contribute to its expansion, as is illustrated by the development of urban light railway systems (Table 3.2) in cities like Manchester (Fig. 3.8), Sheffield and Liverpool (Fig. 3.9) which have had mixed results both in terms of their own profitability and their impact on the urban areas they frequent.

There is no doubt that 'guided people movers' will continue, and perhaps become more important in cities, airports, leisure venues and all urban locations where there is a high density of people. Such technology will include lifts/ elevators, monorails, magnetic levitation, cable ways, trolleybuses, guided bus routes and other such systems.

Automobile technology

Automobile technology, like many other technologies including steam and the rail system, had a slow beginning, but in combination with concrete technology, has eventually come to dominate the development of urban areas in the late

Existing	*First open*
Blackpool Tramway – 18.5 km	1886
Tyne & Wear Metro – 58.5 km, 46 stations	1980
London Docklands Light Rail – 22.6 km, 28 stations	1987
Greater Manchester Metrolink, Phase 1 – 30.9 km, 26 stations	1992
South Yorkshire Supertram, Sheffield – 29 km, 50 stops	1991

With Parliamentary authorization
Midland Metro, Phase 1–21 km, 28 stations
Croydon Tramlink (London), Phase 1–28 km, 36 stations/stops
Leeds Supertram, Phase 1 – 11.9 km
Greater Nottingham Rapid Transit – 14 km, 19 stops

Planned systems
Barking, Belfast (× 2); Brighton, Bristol (× 3); Cardiff, Chelmsford, Chester, Dartford, Dundee, Edinburgh (× 2); Glasgow, Gloucester, Guildford, Haringey, Hartlepool, Kingston-upon-Hull, Kingston-upon-Thames, Lancaster, Liverpool (× 2); London (various), Maidstone, Newcastle/Sunderland, Oxford, Park Royal, Peterborough, Plymouth, Portsmouth, Preston, Royal Docks/London, Reading/Bracknell, Rotherham, Sheffield, Stockport, Stockton (× 2); Stoke on Trent, Stourbridge, Tamworth.

Source: Department of Transport, 1996.

Table 3.2 British light rail/tramway systems

twentieth century (Figs 3.10 and 3.11). The original internal combustion engine was designed in Europe during the latter part of the nineteenth century, and by 1887 Gottlieb Daimler had revolutionized the automobile industry by producing a high-speed internal combustion motor. This became the forerunner to the engine used in most automobiles in the late twentieth century. By the early twentieth century road vehicles, driven by internal combustion engines, were in production, but it was the introduction of another type of technology, the conveyor belt system for manufacturing by Henry Ford in 1913, which significantly increased the use of the motor car. During the same period the General Motors Corporation also began to expand, as did a number of other well-known names in the car industry including John and Horace Dodge and Walter Chrysler. In 1978 the US motor industry had reached an all-time high and was producing 13 million motor vehicle units per year. In 1980 it was estimated that there were 300 million cars and 85 million trucks or buses in operation throughout the world, forming an indispensable transport network.

Inevitably there were worries over oil shortages. Following the Suez Crisis of 1957 there was an oil shortage which was repeated after the Arab–Israeli war of 1973. Despite these problems, the motor industry and automobile technology continued to develop. In 1965 Ralph Nader, an American lawyer and consumer protection advocate, published his book *Unsafe at any Speed* in which he argued that poor automobile design was a major contributor to highway deaths. This resulted in a new set of safety standards, both in America and in other countries across the world. Despite this interruption, the automobile industries continued to grow, particularly with the introduction in the 1980s, by both Ford

Motor Company and General Motors, of the concept of a 'world car' using similar design concepts in a number of plants in a wide range of countries.

The history of the car is the history of urban development in the twentieth century – a trend which is likely to continue into the twenty-first century, despite the fact that 71% of drivers, according to the recent RAC survey, see air pollution and traffic congestion as the greatest problems of road travel. A Lex survey found that 46% of drivers would support improvement to public transport yet few would leave their cars at home if public transport were made

Fig. 3.10. *Concrete and automobile technology. An interstate highway in California, USA.*

Fig. 3.11. *Concrete and automobile technology. The M25 motorway passing through the Green Belt, south-west of London.*

Fig. 3.12. *Automobile technology. Cars queue for parking places in Guildford town centre in 1996.*

Fig. 3.13. *Autobus technology. The bus station in Cardiff, adjacent to the rail station. In some towns and cities park-and-ride bus facilities have successfully enabled the centre to compete with new out-of-town developments.*

Fig. 3.14. Autobus technology. An intercity bus at Milton Keynes, an important part of the public transport infrastructure.

Fig. 3.15. Air transport technology. The approach to Ringway Airport, Manchester, a gateway from towns and cities in north-west England to international markets.

more attractive (Fig. 3.12). Over the last 20 years the number of private cars and vans in Great Britain has increased by almost 50%, as can be seen from Table 3.3.

The impact of cars on urban behaviour is very well illustrated by the National Travel Survey released in 1996 by the Department of Transport (Table 3.4). It charts the enormous growth in car passengers over the last 20 years. However, the use of buses, including park and ride schemes, will be important in the future (Figs 3.13 and 3.14). As an illustration, when the Brent Cross Shopping Centre first opened in north London 20 years ago, there was no bus station. Eventually, when the bus park was created, it contributed to over 30% of all visitors to the shopping centre.

Over the decades cities have adapted to the car, to some extent; Colin Buchanan's report on *Traffic in Towns* in 1963 significantly assisted this process of adaption. The dilemma facing urban areas in the late twentieth century is that the use of cars is both a cause and a product of greater affluence. As affluence advances, so does the desire to travel, but the growth of travel, as we are increasingly aware, destroys the very world we all set out to enjoy. The

	Private cars and vans	All vehicles
1975	13 747	17 501
1980	15 073	19 210
1985	16 453	21 157
1990	19 742	24 673
1995	20 505	25 369

Source: Department of Transport.

Table 3.3 Motor vehicles licensed in Great Britian (1000's)

55

	1975/76	1985/86	1989/91	1993/95
Walk	325	350	328	308
Bicycle	30	25	21	17
Car driver	261	317	387	389
Car passenger	167	200	232	230
Motorcycle	9	9	6	4
British Rail	11	12	12	10
Taxi/minicab	3	7	11	9
All forms	935	1024	1091	1052

Table 3.4 Journeys per person per year

Source: Department of Transport.

challenge is to find a way to enjoy the affluence that technology brings, but spend the wealth in ways which offer an environmentally sustainable future.

Air transport technology

Air transport technology is closely linked to the development of automobile technology. The first air passenger services are believed to have taken place around 1910 when airships moved between different German cities. However, although the Wright brothers made their first historic aeroplane flight in 1904, aeroplane travel did not really start until 1914 in America, although several experimental air mail flights did take place in India, Europe and the United States before the First World War.

By the mid-1920s regular scheduled air mail and passenger flights were beginning to appear in a number of countries. By 1929 Britain was operating a commercial air route to India. This advance in air travel was assisted by improvements in weather forecasting, navigational technology, aerodynamic technology as well as a number of other technological advances in engine design and the development of passenger planes.

During the 1950s turbo prop and jet airliners were replacing rail, road and ocean liners as the primary mode of long-distance travel, but in the 1970s a new generation of wide-bodied or 'jumbo' jets had appeared, as had the Anglo-French Concorde, a supersonic airline operating between United States and Europe.

In the USA a 1978 law deregulated the airline industry and further accelerated the development of 'people carriers' between centres of high-density population. Hub airports developed with a hub and spoke airline system with major airports such as Chicago dominating the network. In Europe, despite the lack of deregulation, a similar network of hub and spoke systems developed with major cities such as London developing hub status. By 1990 it was estimated that there were 925 scheduled airlines, operating around 15 000 aircraft on a daily basis.

Air transport technology has increasingly influenced the winners and losers in the game of urban global competition; all towns and cities are in effect in competition with each other for jobs, residents and consumer expenditure. From any major airport in Britain we can jet away to numerous European destinations for a weekend break and to spend our wealth outside the town of our normal

	Inward	Outward
1980	20 959	21 109
1985	25 958	25 986
1990	37 322	37 301
1995	50 504	50 436

Source: Department of Transport/Civil Aviation Authority.

Table 3.5 UK air passenger movements ('000s)

residence (Fig. 3.15). The growth in air passenger movements in the UK can be seen in Table 3.5.

Electric technology

Electric technology has had, and continues to have, a profound impact on urban development, but not only as a form of power for public transport. Although the ancient Greeks originally discovered static electricity, it was not until 1837 that Michael Faraday developed the electric motor using coils to generate an electromagnetic force, and it was to be another 100 years before this invention began to dominate urban development (such as the rail systems previously mentioned). By 1837 Samuel F.B. Morse had also developed the system of sending telegraphic messages using dots and dashes. Throughout the nineteenth century both these inventions had an influence on urban development. However, it was not until 1876 that Alexander Graham Bell developed the telephone, enabling sound transmission to be passed along lines, from one city to another. At the same time early radio was being developed, but it was not until 1896 that Guglielmo Marchese Marconi sent a wireless signal across the Atlantic. The first US radio broadcast was made a few years later in 1906 and by the 1920s radio networks transmitting programmes had been established in the USA and Europe.

The growth of telephone and radio technology, along with improved transport technology, accelerated the growth of urban areas, but also influenced the shape of these cities. For instance, the growth of the City of London as a major financial world centre would not have been possible without the application of this technology in the twentieth century. In the early twentieth century it was said to be easier to telephone London from Nairobi in Kenya than to telephone Salisbury in what was then neighbouring Southern Rhodesia; all telephone lines led to London!

The first television transmissions took place in 1926. It developed slowly through the 1930s, and it was not until the 1940s, after the Second World War, that the use of this technology accelerated. In 1947, 10 000 television receivers were sold in the USA. In 1948, 190 000 receivers were sold but by 1955 some 32 million had been sold. The growth of satellite and cable transmission is seeing the rise of new moguls able to combine information technology with the growth of leisure. The growth of the Rupert Murdoch and Ted Turner empires, for example, have begun to eclipse the terrestrial broadcasters such as BBC and ITV. The growth of television from the 1920s also ran in parallel with the growth of cinema, eventually resulting in the merger of the two concepts as video tapes, suitable for home viewing, in the 1970s.

In recent years the growth of mobile telephones has been equally impressive. By 1996 it was estimated there were 160 million mobile telephones world wide, a number which is likely to more than double by the year 2000.

Computer technology and the information revolution

Perhaps the most dramatic application of electronic technology has been in the field of computers. In 1944 scientists from Harvard University and MIT in America invented their own programmable computer while the Colossus computer was being developed in Great Britain. Initially IBM and others scoffed at the potential of computers but suddenly embraced the technology during the 1950s. These early computers were not only cumbersome, but they required high-voltage input and generated vast amounts of heat. However, by the 1970s a fourth generation of computers based on microtechnology and microchips had emerged, reducing the cost and improving the productivity of these machines.

Computer technology has moved on dramatically over the years. In the 1970s Wang developed an office-based computer. By 1981 IBM had introduced their own Personal Computer driven by a Microsoft Disk Operating System. IBM eventually realized that the large mainframe computer, originally developed in the 1950s, not only had a limited shelf life but was being copied by a number of other companies, including Amdahl. The IBM/PC was also eventually copied by others such as Compaq, an offshoot of the Texas Instrument Company. However, a few years earlier in the 1970s Digital Computers had produced the Commodore Pet computer using microtechnology and Steve Job had developed the Apple Computer. This product was also driven by software written by Microsoft who, by the 1990s, began to dominate the software market. After growing at 8% a year over the last decade, information technology accounts for almost 3% of GDP in the USA, compared with 2.2% in the UK. The technology sector is having a major influence on stock markets, and Microsoft alone was capitalized at $92 billion in 1996.

The current revolution in computer technology is the advent of the 'information super highway' which will be based, not on 'anolog' form radio waves, but on 'digital' technology. As Bill Gates says in his book *The Road Ahead*:

> Movies, television programmes and all sorts of other digital information will be stored on 'servers' which are computers with spacious disks. Servers will provide information for users anywhere on the network. If you ask to see a particular movie, check a fact or retrieve your electronic mail, your request will be routed by switches to the server or servers storing this information. You won't know whether the material which arrives at your house is stored on a server down the road or on the other side of the country, nor will it matter.
>
> The requested digital data will be retrieved from the server and routed by switches back to your television, personal computer, or telephone – your information appliance. These digital devices will succeed for the same reason that their analog precursors did – they will make some aspect of life easier. Unlike the dedicated word processors that bought the first microprocessors to many offices, these information appliances will be

general purpose, programmable computers connected to the information highway.

It has been suggested that the economic engine of the financial services industry is the production, transformation, distribution and consumption of digital information. Here is the revolution in technology to come which may have a devastating impact on urban developments. Investors in real estate, and politicians concerned at a local and national level barely understand, let alone have anticipated, this technological application. It is a technology which is changing not only the way we work, but also how we communicate with each other. Martin Wolf in the *Financial Times* has suggested that 'changes in technology, and not the competition of developing countries, are the main reasons for growing inequalities in industrialized nations'.

In the same way that economists and urban 'planners' did not anticipate the impact of earlier technological developments, from the use of canals to the use of steam and later the growth in the number of automobiles, urban land use will change out of recognition over the next 20 years.

Telephone technology in the first half of the twentieth century did not cause the dispersal of population, but accelerated the polarization of employment into certain geographic areas. The advent of the Internet and the information superhighway will also polarize urban activity (Fig. 3.16). However, the forces causing this polarization, and the shape of urban areas, will be different to the application of earlier technologies. In recent months the focus has been on JAVA, a programming language by James Gosling at Sun Microsystems in 1990. This may transform the use of the World Wide Web and break the fixed links between the application and operating system. Programs in future will run on any computed platform via the Inter or Intra Net and will eventually link up with television.

Fig. 3.16. Information technology. An example of a recent urban development, combining the use of the Internet with a restaurant, both growth sectors of the economy.

Programme transmission

In the history of economic thought it is rare to find technology taken seriously. The article 'Technology and unemployment' which appeared in the *The Economist* (11 February 1995) is a rarity. The article posed the question: 'Technology, especially information technology is destroying millions of jobs. The hope is that it will create more than it destroys. Will it?' However, as Professor Jeremy Rifkin has said in his prophetic book *The End of Work*:

> The Information Age has arrived. In the years ahead, new, more sophisticated software technologies are going to bring civilisation even closer to a near-workless world. In the agricultural, manufacturing and service sectors, machines are quickly replacing human labour and promise an economy of near automated production by the mid decade of the twenty-first century. Redefining opportunities and responsibilities for millions of people in a society absent of mass formal employment is likely to be the single most pressing social issue of the coming century.

The onward march of technology is ruthless and unending. Those involved with urban property investment and urban planning (land management) need to gain a far better understanding of the technology typhoon which is fast approaching. We need to reflect on Lewis Mumford's words when he says that a city is a '. . . ceremonial meeting place that serves as the goal for pilgrimage. . .' .

CHAPTER 4

The spending zone for affluence?

The history of urban land use for 45 years, until 1990, was characterized by an intensification of retail use within town centres. As far as retailing is concerned, many town planners have their minds set in the past which they appear to wish to preserve, and have an inability to understand or anticipate the future. Retailing activity within many town and city centres will continue to decline in the decade ahead, and even if middle-income housing returns to town centres, the resulting expenditure will not arrest the decline.

Some investors and developers are similarly myopic; most rarely fully anticipate the future, although they are obviously investing for future pecuniary returns. Nevertheless, a few investors and developers, and the more successful retailers, continue to demonstrate an ability to adapt to change, meeting evolving consumer tastes and remaining profitable.

The announcements from Secretaries of State for the Environment that we should either 'let the market decide' (as stated during the 1980s) and permit more out-of-town development, or 'restrict out-of-town development and protect town centres' (as has been suggested during the 1990s) have had little impact on the long-term trends. The trend to out-of-town development has been gathering momentum over more than two decades; successive Secretaries of State for the Environment did not cause it to happen during the 1980s, and the trend in the late 1990s cannot be stopped. Indeed, by trying to prevent out-of-town development in the late 1990s, the Secretary of State for the Environment may be accelerating the trends away from town centres, making retailers and developers think that the restriction on the supply of land out of town is likely to increase its value. This may have the impact of raising both awareness and expectations, and thereby encouraging yet more investments in out-of-town locations.

When the then Prime Minister Margaret Thatcher, on the night of her re-election in 1987, stood at the door of No.10 Downing Street and said that we must pay more attention to the inner cities, she was totally correct. The future success and many of the problems of mature countries like Great Britain, in a globally competitive world, depend on the future of all its towns and cities. But it is the lack of a political solution, and the inability to think laterally about the problem, which means that the issue today is no better than it was a decade ago. Giving favourable treatments to rural retail business, by adjustments to the Uniform Business Rate, as promoted in 1996, might please the Council for the Protection of Rural England but is unlikely to assist retailing in inner cities and town centres generally.

Town centre management has been accepted as a concept for some years and in some towns is now firmly in practice. There is now an Association of Town Centre Managers; however, this is primarily seen as a way of maintaining the retail status quo, or even increasing town centre retail activity. The loyalty card, recently introduced by shop keepers in Leominster, giving customers a discount for shopping in the town, and the calls for a new system of mandatory funding of American-style Town Improvement Zones by the private sector, reflect this desire. Town centres as locations for intense retail activity, creating traffic problems, road congestion and the need for ever more car parking space (all implying environmental problems), are relatively recent developments. They are a response to the growth of affluence and the application of technology during the last 50 years – especially car ownership. The use of town and city centres in this way is unique to the twentieth century and does not automatically imply that such intensive land use is the solution to an environmentally sustainable future.

James Morrell, the well-known economic forecaster who is credited with having set up The Henley Centre for Forecasting, has frequently stated: 'What the rich do today creates the appetite of the masses in the future.' This brief statement summarizes the growth of retail expenditure in the post-Second World War era. Luxuries such as televisions, refrigerators, cars and holidays – many involving international travel – have become commonplace for the majority of the population in such mature economies as Great Britain. The growth of travel is a direct result of greater affluence. Unless environmentally friendly ways of spending this affluence can be found, the trend towards even greater mobility is likely to continue, bringing environmental problems in its wake.

The 1950s

In the early years after the Second World War two events conspired to inhibit urban change: the lack of consumer expenditure following the wartime auster-ities, and the central government's lack of understanding of property markets in a democratic economy. One of the features of the Town and Country Planning Act 1947 was to impose a development charge of 100% on the increasing value of land resulting from new developments. This was the first of several attempts over several decades to tax development land values. However, if production is to take place in a 'market economy', a surplus or profit must be produced; in other words, the sale price realized by a product must be greater than the cost of producing that product. In a 'planned economy', such as existed in the old Soviet Union, where production is dictated by a hegemony, market forces are normally unimportant as a way of determining people's wishes.

With the assistance of Marshall Aid from the USA, the UK, together with other western European countries, returned relatively quickly to economic health in the 1940s. The rising level of affluence caused an increase in demand for new buildings, including shops. The imposition of a development charge of 100%, and the need for building licences made land owners naturally reluctant to release land for development. The supply of building land became restricted and the price of land increased. Following the change of government in 1951, the development charge provision was abolished in 1953. By November 1954 building licences were also revoked. Although the 1950s were characterized by a series of credit squeezes, with bank base rates frequently being increased and a few years later being reduced (as shown by Table 7.2 later), the decade saw substantial new retail development.

The history of this period of urban development is documented in Oliver Marriott's book *The Property Boom*, in which he charts the abilities of a number of property entrepreneurs to rebuild Britain's cities, still devastated by the efforts of wartime bombing. From Liverpool to Exeter, and from South-ampton to Coventry, entrepreneurs reconstructed town centres. They also became successful as manipulators of the property market, realizing substantial pecuniary gains. As Marriott records, Charles Clore achieved fame as one of the original and successful asset-strippers. In January 1950 he purchased Sears, a company which was still valued at its pre-Second World War level totalling £2.3 million. Despite a quick revaluation of the properties by the shareholders to a new value of £6 million, the takeover was completed. However, Mr Clore then sold a group of shops for £4.5 million and took leasebacks. The Legal & General Assurance Company became the landlord and the leases were held in the trading name of Freeman Hardy & Willis. Mr Clore still owned freehold property, which he retained, worth £4 million, and was then able to proceed to invest in other town centre developments.

The property entrepreneurs of the 1950s were feeding a growing need; with rising spending power, the increasing urbanization of the population and the growth of car ownership, retail expenditure became increasingly polarized away from villages towards town and city centres. The decade also saw the birth of self-service stores.

From 1950 onwards, there was a period of two decades during which town centres were rebuilt, but the problems of car ownership began to emerge as both a benefit and a nuisance. In the 1960s Colin Buchanan was commissioned by the government to produce his now famous report *Traffic in Towns*, which suggested how street patterns could be managed to accommodate the growth in motorized road technology. This period was also characterized by early attempts to pedestrianize retail streets. One of the earliest streets to be pedestrianized was Montague Street in Worthing, but here, as with other streets, the initial reaction from retailers was negative; they feared that they would lose trade by reducing consumers' ability to access their shop fronts. As history has later been able to prove, the majority of pedestrianization schemes have been beneficial to retailers and rental values steadily increased in pedestrianized zones until the late 1980s (Figs. 4.1, 4.2 and 4.3). Some commentators have even gone as far as to suggest that pedestrianization caused excessive rental growth; an alternative view is that town planners only pedestrianized those areas of town centres which were most popular with the retailing public. In other words, intense retail expenditure polarized into town and city centres, and improvements in rental values in certain streets resulting from such expenditure, caused pedestrianization!

The in-town retail property booms

During the 1960s a number of purpose-built shopping centres began to appear, modelled on similar concepts in America. The Whitgift Centre in Croydon was one of the pioneering developments, built on the site of the Old Whitgift Grammar School which was relocated to the edge of Croydon. The Arndale Shopping Centres created during this period were other examples of entrepreneurial developments. A combination of Arnold Hagenbach's and Sam Chippindale's name, Arndale's were developed in a large number of towns including Manchester, Wandsworth, Luton and many more. Without the intensification of retail activity in town centres, such developments would not have been possible.

The Elephant & Castle retail development in south London and the Bull Ring in Birmingham also characterized the revolution in shopping centres in the early 1960s. While the Elephant & Castle has not generally been regarded as a success, the Bull Ring in its early days brought retailers back into the centre of Birmingham, which throughout the 1950s had remained an extensive Second World War bomb site. Another success was the County Square in Ashford, Kent, shown in Fig. 4.4.

Urban redevelopment was not always a success; not only was the Elephant & Castle development of very mixed merit but, in towns as far apart as Portsmouth and Derby, bricks were laid and concrete poured which did not justify their investment value. The 1947 Planning Act had not anticipated, or 'planned' such developments, and the entrepreneurs relied on intuition rather than serious research before committing substantial sums of money to such schemes. The politics of urban development means that, even in the late 1990s, such haphazard decisions by both physical town planners and property investors and developers continue.

A very different procedure was adopted for the development of the Brent Cross Shopping Centre on the North Circular in London near Wembley. Here serious research was undertaken not only into the physical form of the development but also into its locations in relation to road access and its residential hinterlands. Brent Cross copied many of the concepts from purpose-built shopping malls that already existed in North America during the 1960s, and even today it is regarded as an investment success story and continues to be popular with the shopping public. The two-level approach, with car access to the rear and bus station access (at a lower level) at the front, have resulted in a three-dimensional flow of pedestrians throughout the schemes.

Fig. 4.1. *The pedestrianization of Buchanan Street has been the saviour of Glasgow. It has continued to attract some of the major names in international retailing in recent years.*

Fig. 4.2. *The pedestrianization of the cobbled High Street in Guildford has made the town a popular location for leisure-oriented retailing. Guildford won the British Council for Shopping Centres' Town Centre Environment Award in 1996.*

Fig. 4.3. *The pedestrianization of Queen Street, Cardiff links a number of retail traders within the heart of the city.*

Fig. 4.4. *County Square, Ashford, Kent. The 1960s Tufton Centre was refurbished in the 1980s to maintain its competitive edge. The centre was enclosed, car park upgraded and lighting plus entrances improved. (Photograph: Damond Lock Grabowski & Partners.)*

In France during this period Jean Louis Solal, the father of French Shopping Centres, also introduced this American style of retail development, resulting in a number of centres being built around Paris such as Creteil Soleil, Parly Deux and Velizy Deux.

The foodstore boom

The 1970s onwards has been characterized by the development of out-of-town foodstores. One of the earliest was the Carrefour store near Chandlers Ford, Eastleigh near Southampton (Fig. 4.5), now owned by Asda. Similar stores were built at Caerphilly in Wales and at Patchway near Bristol (Fig. 4.6); at this time Tesco also developed a similar large store at Irlam, Manchester and Sainsbury created a scheme on the edge of Cambridge. These large foodstores were different in two respects from in-town foodstores, which had often been used to 'anchor' in-town shopping centre developments. These 'hypermarkets' were freestanding with their own adjacent car parking and often contained in excess of 5000 m^2 of retail floorspace. What is now considered commonplace was a novelty when the Eastleigh Hypermarket was opened in 1974, on a site of 5 hectares containing a total floor area of 12–400 m^2 of which 5000 m^2 was for sales split 40/60 between food and non-food items. Car parking of more than 800 spaces, together with a cheap petrol station, was regarded as extraordinary at the time, but pointed the way to the future.

The Unit for Retail Planning Information in Reading has tracked the growth of this type of retail development, which was neither planned nor anticipated by town planners (Fig. 4.7). The number of hypermarkets and superstores in Great

Fig. 4.5. The Asda foodstore at Chandlers Ford near Southampton. Formerly Carrefour, one of the first hypermarkets constructed in the 1970s. (Photograph: Asda Stores.)

Britain has steadily increased from less than 20 in 1970 to well over 700 in the 1990s (Table 4.1). Such extraordinary growth in this form of retailing could not have been possible without the growth of car ownership over the last three decades. By the late 1980s it was estimated that more than 80% of the country's population had access to (or was able to drive) a car. In addition to road technology, electronics – in the form of electronic point of sale and laser scanners – has accelerated the improvements in retail productivity. The Unit for Retail Planning Information has divided consumer expenditure into two broad categories: convenience goods covering food, alcoholic drinks, tobacco plus other weekly goods such as newspapers; and comparison goods covering clothing, DIY material, household goods, recreational goods (such as televisions) and other items, including pharmaceuticals. Over the years they have observed the changes in consumer expenditure presented in Table 4.2.

The growth of consumer expenditure on convenience goods has been relatively modest. What has changed urban retail development and encouraged the growth of food stores has been greater mobility, not an increase in expenditure. As has been frequently suggested, there is a limit to how much anyone can eat! However, there is no limit to how or where you buy food in the

Fig. 4.6. The Asda foodstore at Patchway near Cribbs Causeway, Bristol. It opened as Carrefour in the 1970s and sowed the seed for a new out-of-town retail district with a catchment population stretching up and down the M4 and M5 motorways. (Photograph: Asda Stores.)

Fig. 4.7. Inside an Asda foodstore on Merseyside; a cornucopia of produce from all over the world, a retail consumer success story not anticipated by town planners.

age of automobile technology. The history of retail expenditure and property development in the post-Second World War until the mid-1980s was characterized by a polarization of retail expenditure, either to town centres (for goods generally) or to major foodstores (as with convenience expenditure).

Comparison expenditure, as illustrated in Table 4.2, has grown in real terms much faster over the last three decades with the advance of material affluence. It is this expenditure growth which has changed town centres so dramatically in the post-war era. In 1985 Alan Tate, one of the leading planning consultants of that decade, said:

	Superstores (2500–4999m^2)		Hypermarkets (5000m^2)		Total cumulative trading floorspace (m^2)
	No. opened in year	Cumulative total	No. opened in year	Cumulative total	
1970	7	13	0	1	51 500
1975	11	61	2	7	250 900
1980	17	143	4	24	637 700
1985	33	274	1	38	1 148 400
1990	67	576	4	51	2 258 800
1994	64	823	2	62	3 138 200
Planned @ 1995	83	–	6	–	= extra 311 400

Table 4.1 Hypermarkets and superstores by year of opening

Source: The Unit for Retail Planning Information, Reading.

Year	Convenience goods	Comparison goods	All goods
1971	£891	£602	£1486
1981	£904	£786	£1689
1991	£1080	£1194	£2276
1994	£1137	£1295	£2431
Average real growth, p.a. (index 1990) 1971–94	+1.2%	+3.5%	+2.3%

Table 4.2 Retail expenditure growth (annual, per customer)

Source: Unit for Retail Planning Information, Reading.

The ability of the planning system in this country to adapt to the changes underway in the retail sector is being questioned. As appeals over the development of edge or out-of-town superstores have became more common, the stretches and strains inherent in town planning has become more and more evident.

By 1971 the appropriateness of existing town planning policy was being called into question. This is ironic because the Town and Country Planning Act of 1968 introduced, for the first time, the concept of strategic Structure Plans which establish the main guidelines for controls development in planning areas. These were to be complemented by Local Plans prepared by local authorities. The reality was that the Structure Plans were not published until the mid or late 1970s and some did not even appear until the 1980s after many of the large foodstores had already been built. The failure of Structure Plans to provide adequately for emerging forms of retail development led to widespread conflicts between retailers seeking to satisfy the requirements of shoppers on the one hand, and planning authorities seeking to preserve 'traditional' shopping patterns on the other. The fact that shopping patterns of the 1970s and 1980s were unlike previous decades, and not 'traditional', was often overlooked. Well-structured, but 'non-traditional' shopping areas can be seen in Figs 4.8, 4.9 and 4.10.

By the late 1980s most Structure and Local Planning policies generally realized the need to support superstores with adequate car parking, but this was also after many other forms of out-of-town retailing had been constructed. In 1988 Brent Cross (if one excludes the purpose-built covered shopping centre in Milton Keynes new town constructed in 1985) was then the single example of a purpose-built subregional centre in the whole of the British Isles. Its performance had been carefully monitored by both consultants, and the then Greater London Council, and had indicated no long-term adverse effect on shopping, as it was believed it had simply been able to absorb the growth in retail expenditure. As Alan Tate said in 1985:

> Nevertheless, no Structure Plan anywhere in the British Isles makes any provision for the establishment for a new subregional centre to complement existing traditional retailing facilities. Proposals for such centres

Fig. 4.8. Inside the Friary Centre, Guildford. A clean, managed shopping environment which has been upgraded in recent years.

Fig. 4.9. Inside the St Enoch shopping centre in the centre of Glasgow; a retail success story which is likely to remain popular as a city centre destination.

Fig. 4.10. The clean, safe and managed shopping environment at the St David's Centre, Cardiff, gives a focal point to retailing in the Welsh capital.

will therefore need to be considered on the basis that they are - by definition - in conflict with established policies.

The history of retail development over the last half century reflects the problem with town planning. By the mid-1980s it was clear that the shopping public enjoyed out-of-town shopping, and by that date Marks & Spencer and other retailers such as the John Lewis Partnership had already publicized the fact that they were seeking edge-of-town locations.

The *laissez-faire* 1980s

The 1980s saw the most dramatic change in planning policy of the last half century; the government of the day introduced Enterprise Zones, as well as

Fig. 4.11. The Merry Hill Centre at Brierley Hill in the West Midlands, a retail and leisure destination with its own internal railway linking different areas of the development. (Photograph: The Merry Hill Centre.)

Urban Development Corporations (UDCs) based upon the successful New Town Corporations of the immediate post-war era. The concept behind both these initiatives was to free up the land market and create urban renewal. The Local Government, Planning and Land Act 1980 set out the objectives of UDCs.

> The objective of an Urban Development Corporation shall be to secure the regeneration of its area, by bringing land and buildings into affective use, encouraging the development of existing and new industry and commerce, creating an attractive environment and ensuring that housing and social facilities are available to encourage people to live and work in the area.

The result was dramatic; in a matter of five years four major new out-of-town purpose-built shopping centres (similar to Brent Cross in north London) had been built on derelict urban land, although not all were within UDCs. The Metro Centre near Gateshead, Newcastle, was developed by Cameron Hall and the Church Commissioners containing 2.2 million ft^2, Merry Hill Shopping Centre near Dudley in the West Midlands (Fig. 4.11) was developed by

Fig. 4.12. The Meadowhall Shopping Centre near Sheffield, one of the most successful shopping centres of the 1980s, constructed on reclaimed land formerly occupied by a steel works.

Richardson Developments to contain 1.8 million ft^2, Meadowhall was developed on the edge of Sheffield by Stadium Developments/Eddie Healey creating 1.8 million ft^2 (Figs. 4.12 and 4.13), and Lakeside was developed in East London near Thurrock by Capital and Counties (now Capital Shopping Centres) to contain 1.15 million ft^2 (Fig. 4.14). These larger regional shopping centres have consolidated their position at the upper end of the list of the most successful retail locations in Great Britain (Table 4.3).

These developments, as well as numerous smaller out-of-town retail warehouse developments such as Fosse Park near Leicester and Beta Value, Harlesden (Fig. 4.15), aimed to meet two different objectives. They accommodated both the growth in retail expenditure and shoppers' wishes to drive to well-designed retail facilities, but many also aimed to renovate run-down urban areas. Many achieved both of these objectives, but they also accelerated the process of urban change, causing a major structural shift away from traditional town centres as the location for intense retail activity.

Fig. 4.13. Inside the Meadowhall Shopping Centre, a clean, managed, landscaped environment. (Photograph: Meadowhall Centre Limited.)

Fig. 4.14. The Lakeside Shopping Centre, Thurrock. Although it took a few months to establish itself, it has become one of the dominant retail and leisure destinations on the east side of London. (Photograph: Thurrock Lakeside, Capital Shopping Centres Plc.)

The structural shift continues

This structural shift in retail activity is demonstrated by patterns of retail rental growth (Fig. 4.16). For three decades or more rental values in the centre of cities steadily increased, reflecting the polarization of retail activity in these locations. From 1980 onwards, however, out-of-town warehouse retailing became established, although a number of retail warehouses initially opened in

	1992	1993	1994	1995
Metro Centre, Gateshead	11	5	2	1
Meadowhall, Sheffield	16	3	1	2
Lakeside, Thurrock	34	9	10	3
Princes Street, Edinburgh	5	2	6	4
Merry Hill, Dudley	28	10	3	5
Oxford Street, London	1	1	4	6

Table 4.3 Ranked by sales per m²

Source: DTZ Debenham Thorpe Research/Property Managers Association, 1996.

empty cinemas and similar buildings. In the early years rental values were often linked to the rental values for warehouse-industrial buildings; however, by the mid-1980s retail warehouse rents were being openly negotiated in the market-place (Fig. 4.17). Table 4.4 shows that although rental values for in-town retail stores and out-of-town retail warehouse buildings increased dramatically in the boom years of the late 1980s (reaching a peak in 1988), when in-town retail rents started to fall during the recession in the 1990s, most retail warehouse rents, throughout this period continued to increase. In other words, even the recession of the early 1990s was not sufficient to reverse the continuing structural shift in retail activity away from town centres to edge-of-town locations.

With reference to the development of retail warehouse parks, a number of commentators have suggested that out-of-town retail development will continue; there are so many retail warehouse park schemes 'in the pipeline' (Table 4.5) that in the short term (as well as the long term) physical town planning policies are unlikely to be effective.

The success of out-of-town retail development during the recession of the early 1990s (for example, the Boots development shown in Fig. 4.18) resulted in the government rethinking town centre planning policy. This rethink resulted in the revised *Planning Policy Guidance Note 6* (PGG6), issued in June 1996. This set out clear guidance:

– On planning for town centres and retailing, with an emphasis on a plan led approach . . . selecting sites for development (including leisure).
– On the promotion of mixed use developments in town centres, including the promotion of town centre managers . . . including attractive and secure car parks.
– On the assessment of research proposals relating to the impact on vitality and viability, accessibility by choice of transport and the impact on travel and car use, with a reference to how out of town centre developments should be assessed.

This document suggested that Local Plans and Unitary Developments Plans (introduced for metropolitan areas in the 1980s) should consider existing provision and 'identify sites for development'. In this one simple phase is the on-going problem: How can a physical planning system second guess the property market in a dynamic market economy? Over the last 50 years it has produced an extremely poor track record.

Fig. 4.15. Beta Value, Harlesden. A discrete mini-retail-park development on back land with good road access to both parking and the high street, able to complete with out-of-town retailing. (Photograph: Damond Lock Grabowski & Partners.)

Fig. 4.16. Bond Street, London, where rental values have increased much faster than inflation in recent years reflecting the polarization of wealth, and a leisure–retail destination for the more affluent.

Fig. 4.17. The Ladymead Retail Park on the edge of Guildford accommodates retailers who cannot trade successfully within the medieval town centre.

Fig. 4.18. Boots on the Wirral Leisure Park. Almost all major established retailers now trade in out-of-town locations. In recent years Boots the Chemists have experimented with non-high street locations.

	REMI retail (%)	IPD retail (%)	REMI retail warehouse (%)	IPD retail warehouse (%)
1980	–	19.66	44.93	–
1981	9.10	7.74	10.03	5.40
1982	5.90	5.20	2.45	6.70
1983	4.90	2.89	–0.31	–2.00
1984	7.00	6.43	6.31	8.70
1985	9.40	9.17	12.55	9.50
1986	9.60	9.24	4.79	8.80
1987	14.50	20.21	6.70	11.90
1988	19.40	22.81	20.73	13.70
1989	14.40	11.26	9.14	8.90
1990	4.60	2.13	3.45	1.50
1991	–2.00	–3.07	–0.96	2.00
1992	–3.30	–6.11	2.06	2.40
1993	–2.10	–4.98	1.98	4.50
1994	–0.70	–0.71	2.17	2.50
1995	1.20	0.06	3.07	4.10
1996	3.00	–	5.70	–

Table 4.4 Rental value growth per year

Source: Investment Property Databank, 1996, and Richard Ellis Monthly Index.

A current issue relates to the size of retail units. Many retailers cannot find a sufficiently large unit in town centres. For those who stay in town their requirement for a standard unit has changed from a grid of 5.4 m (18 ft) frontage with a depth of 18.3 m (60 ft) to a module of 7.6 m (25 ft) by 33.5 m (110 ft).

The dynamic nature of economic change always results in the market identifying opportunities which the town planning process does not anticipate. Although the government's planning brief suggests that, where an out-of-centre site is proposed for retail development 'the onus will be on the developer to demonstrate that he has thoroughly assessed all potential town centre options', there is an on-going dilemma: How should one reconcile this conflict? In many edge-of-town or out-of-town locations across Great Britain there are sites where there was considerable opposition during the planning consideration process, often referred to as the NIMBY problem: Not In My Back Yard. However, when the new retail facility has been created, the shopping and voting public

	Proposed	With planning consent	Under construction	Total pipeline
September 1992	0.76	1.45	0.12	2.33
September 1993	0.68	1.46	0.33	2.47
September 1994	1.39	1.58	0.25	3.22
September 1995	1.24	1.76	0.23	3.23

Table 4.5 Retail warehouse parks (million m²)

Source: Hillier Parker.

have used the facility with great enthusiasm, despite their apparent political objection to the development when proposed! It is also widely recognized that many out-of-town centre retail developments have been constructed in areas of urban deprivation and have already contributed towards urban regeneration.

PPG6, which aims to resolve these conflicts, is linked with PPG 13, which concerns transport issues. When issued in March 1994, this document stated:

> The government is committed to increasing the real level of fuel duty by on average at least 5% a year ... Development plans should aim to reduce the need to travel, especially by car. A major element of this framework, as set out in the sustainable development strategy, is to encourage people to take full account of the wider cost of their transport choice, such as the impact on the environment.

One of the dilemma's all land-use planners face is that the increased use of cars, and the road network, is a result of greater affluence, and that this greater affluence has had a symbiotic relationship with the growth of automobile technology! More car ownership has encouraged car usage, which in itself has improved the level of overall affluence. Until government at a local, national and international level is able to solve this dilemma, Planning Policy Guidance Notes aimed at reducing car usage, however well intentioned, are unlikely to stem the tide of motorized technology and its influence on human behaviour.

In 1996 there were a large number of major out-of-town retail schemes with planning permission, either proposed or under construction. These included the Trafford Centre to be built at Dumplington near Manchester, the Cribbs Causeway development outside Bristol, the Bluewater Retail Park to be built in north Kent, The Fort retail park in north-east Birmingham, Braehead Park in Govan, Glasgow, the White Rose Centre outside Leeds and the White City development on the west side of Greater London. All these schemes, and many other smaller retail warehouse schemes, are likely to be constructed over the next decade, despite the government's apparent preferred option for town centre retail developments. Many will be seen as catalysts to urban regeneration. For instance, the Bluewater Retail Park, which has a catchment population of 9 million residents within an hour's drive, is likely to generate 7000 jobs during the three-year construction period and a further 6800 jobs in the centre itself, and within the industries servicing it when it opens.

The impact of out-of-town shopping facilities, which are clearly very popular with the shopping public, will have a mixed effect on traditional town centre retailing. As Russell Schiller, referring to a major survey of national retailer representation in trading locations, says:

> The proximity of large and successful out of town regional centres tends to lead to a decline in a town centre's ranking, but the effect is complex. The results confirm that successful town-centre retail development can go a long way to alleviate this effect.

Table 4.6 shows that towns such as Dagenham, Grays, Gateshead, Dudley, West Bromwich, Sheffield and Doncaster have suffered and are now ranked lower in the pecking order of popularity; other towns have not. Table 4.7 shows that towns such as Aberdeen and Woking have benefited from new in-town development and are now ranked higher than in 1989. The demand for out-of-town retail units continues. The annual FOCUS survey (Table 4.8) reveals a much stronger demand for out-of-town units in many locations. More than the 10 towns out of the 50 surveyed also showed that the gross level of demand fell by over 100 000 ft^2 between 1995 and 1996.

The trend towards out-of-town retailing, where it is estimated more than 30% of all retail spend now takes place, was reflected in the University of Salford/Richard Ellis survey of leading retail investors: 40% favoured leisure/

	Rank in 1984	Rank in 1989	Rank in 1995
Lakeside: opened 1990			
Romford	46	53	51
Dagenham	307	354	541
Grays	241	300	385
Basildon	89	59	71
Metro Centre: opened 1986			
Newcastle	8	9	15
Sunderland	53	92	64
Durham	204	142	160
Gateshead	335	414	658
Merry Hill: opened 1986–89			
Birmingham	2	3	4
Wolverhampton	16	22	54
Dudley	74	142	209
West Bromwich	110	171	209
Meadowhall: opened 1989			
Sheffield	9	15	23
Barnsley	97	78	106
Rotherham	166	142	209
Doncaster	39	38	61

Table 4.6 Effect of major centres on town centre rank

Source: Hillier Parker Research, 1996.

	Rank in 1984	Rank in 1989	Scheme	Rank in 1995
Aberdeen	26	33	Bon Accord – 1990	9
Bromley	37	48	The Glades – 1991	24
Kingston	31	29	Bentalls – 1992	18
Watford	39	59	Harlequin – 1990	33
Woking	137	153	The Peacocks – 1992	96

Table 4.7 Effects of in-town schemes on town centre rank

Source: Hillier Parker Research, 1996

	Total	In-town	Out-of-town
Birmingham	1299	543	756
Leeds	1162	527	635
Manchester	1129	519	610
Newcastle-upon-Tyne	1013	499	514
Cambridge	979	521	458
Bristol	963	384	579

Table 4.8 Focus on retail demand: top six towns 1996 ('000s ft².)

Source: Property Intelligence, 1996.

retail parks, 35% retail warehouses, 19% shopping centres but only 4% in-town retail units as the location for new investment monies.

The dilemma for town centres

The dilemma for town centres is quite simply: What is their future? The answer is to be found partly in the leisure industry (Fig. 4.19) and partly in the food industry (Figs. 4.20 and 4.21). As economies mature over time, from hunter-gathering economies, to agrarian economies, to industrial economies and on to become service industry economies, a smaller and smaller percentage of workforce is committed to basic 'life-supporting' employment. In other words, fewer and fewer people are required, with the advance of technology, in the agricultural sector, manufacturing sector and, in the late 1990s, in the financial service sector.

The schedule of household expenditure presented in Table 4.9 clearly shows the trend. The advent of legal Sunday trading is part of the trend towards leisure retailing, with some stores, particularly out of town, enjoying sales in excess of 30% of their peak Saturday figures. Linked to the advance in technology is the issue of electronic retailing. Barry Wood at the University of Newcastle upon

Fig. 4.19. The Griffin, Kingston-upon-Thames. The renovation of an historic building in Kingston Market, formerly a coaching inn and later a public house. Its renovation retains a cultural heritage yet reflects the evolution of the town centre. (Photograph: Damond Lock Grabowski & Partners.)

Tyne and others have studied this issue, considering: Just-in-Time delivery, teleshopping, Modex cards, telephone sales, computer databases, CCTV, electronic tagging and Internet/e-mail. They concluded that retail occupiers and developers/investors do not appear worried by the potential impact of information technology (IT) on their businesses:

> Use of IT certainly enables retailers to allocate more of their floorspace to retail use and less to storage. ... Developments in EPOS (Electronic Point of Sale) and JiT (Just in Time) delivery imply that accessibility is critical if city centres are to complete with out of town locations.

A counter-view has been expressed by others considering the impact of the Internet on shopping. For instance, Nigel Cope in *The Independent* suggested:

> Some retailers are more vulnerable than others. People will still prefer to go shopping to try on clothes, sit on furniture and hear expensive TV and audio equipment. But what about commodity items such as books and records? In CDs, for example, it is the artist that is the brand, not the retailer. What value is the retailer adding? ... Supermarkets also look

Fig. 4.20. (top left) The St David's Market, opened in 1987, adding interest and diversity to retailing in central Cardiff.

Fig. 4.21. (top right) The street market in North Street, Guildford, remains popular although it has suffered recently with competition from several out-of-town foodstores.

Fig. 4.22. (bottom left) A farmers' retail outlet in Pennsylvania, USA. As in Great Britain, car boot sales, pick your own farms and garden centres have become popular with the car-owning leisure-oriented public. Such land uses compete with town and city centres for retail expenditure.

vulnerable. They represent a time-consuming distress-purchase that indi-viduals would prefer to avoid. Home shopping could prove attractive to those prepared to pay extra for home delivery.

Home delivery is also an old idea, but it costs money. Cullens, the family grocer, declined in the 1960s at a moment when another family grocer, J. Sainsbury, expanded. Cullens remained with home delivery (often by telephone orders) yet J. Sainsbury expanded using self-service and cost/price efficiency.

	Indices at constant prices (1990 = 100)					£ billion (current prices)	Change % 1971–94
	1971	1981	1986	1991	1994	1994	
Housing	68	81	93	100	104	66.6	52
Motor vehicle	48	62	83	91	101	52.9	110
Food	87	91	95	100	104	47.4	19
Recreation and cultural services	31	58	76	99	112	37.2	261
Catering	56	58	73	93	96	36.9	71
Household goods and services	59	68	85	98	111	27.2	88
Alcohol	73	93	98	96	95	25,8	39
Clothing and footwear	52	67	92	100	114	24.7	119
Monetary services	27	36	68	99	101	16.9	274
Fuel, light and power	86	94	103	108	107	14.9	24
Other travel	67	71	84	97	103	14.0	53
Tobacco	136	121	101	98	86	11.0	–37
Post and telecommunications	33	63	80	100	115	7.9	248
Books, newspaper and magazines	101	97	92	95	97	5.4	–4
Other goods and services	26	54	72	98	97	29.3	273
Less expenditure by foreign tourists, etc.	48	72	94	86	104	–11.3	116
Household expenditure abroad	34	66	78	97	130	13.8	282
All household expenditure	59	72	85	98	104	420.4	76

Source: Office for National Statistics.

Table 4.9 Household expenditure United Kingdom Index (1900 = 100)

All these issues are not new but an advancement of electronic technology. Shopping remains a social experience, including window shopping, and for some in society it is one of the few social experiences they enjoy, particularly for the unemployed or retired. The growth and popularity of weekend car boot sales also runs counter to the idea that electronics will replace retailing. The Covent Garden phenomenon, and the growth of Festival Shopping in other parts of the world, suggests that 'leisure retailing' is with us for at least another millennium (Fig. 4.22).

The announcement by Waterstones in 1996, owned by the WH Smith retail group, that they intended to open a book superstore in Glasgow, fits this trend. The envisaged 25 000 ft^2 store will stock not only 150 000 books but also magazines, newspapers, computer software, videos and a coffee bar/restaurant. King's Walk, Chelsea, offers a similar shopping, eating and leisure time experience (Fig. 4.23) as does The Shires, Leamington Spa (Fig. 4.24) and the Friary Centre, Guildford (Fig. 4.25).

Fig. 4.23. King's Walk, Kings Road, Chelsea. A shopping, eating and leisure time experience which is part of Kings Road – a place both to see and to be seen in. (Photograph: Damond Lock Grabowski & Partners.)

Catering for a leisured society is becoming big business. Roughly one-third of all meals in the USA are now eaten out. In the UK only 1 meal in 16 is eaten outside the home, but the trend is now towards USA-style catering. The Institute of Employment Research estimates that, by 2001, 6.3% of all employment will be based in the hotel and catering industry, which is only part of the leisure industry. Major companies now vie for trade such as Bright Reason with their Bella Pasta and Pizzaland chains, Whitbread with Beefeater and Pizza Hut formats, Pizza Express, McDonald's, Burger King, Kentucky Fried Chicken,

Fig. 4.24. The Shires, Leamington Spa, combining the image of leisure uses and the use of the car park in the evening with better quality destination shopping facilities. (Photograph: Damond Lock Grabowski & Partners.)

Fig. 4.25. The provision of eating facilities within the Friary Centre, Guildford, adds to its attractiveness as a retail location within a subregional shopping town.

and other names. Major brewers, including Bass, J.D. Weatherspoon, Boddington, Scottish & Newcastle, consider leisure eating to be just as important as drinking for their future success.

By the late 1980s it was estimated that over 90% of all employees were entitled to four weeks leave or more per year, compared with a standard of around two weeks in the 1950s. In 1990 around 17–18% of all employees already worked formal flexi-time. As leisure time grows, the leisure industrial sector will also grow quickly.

Table 4.9 shows how the pattern of expenditure has changed since the 1970s. In real terms, the amount of money spent on books, newspapers and magazines has hardly changed over more than three decades, and has fallen in terms of tobacco expenditure. However, the growth in affluence has resulted in all other sectors showing increased levels of expenditure. Even food shows a very modest increase, as people have opted for luxury foods, such as prepared meals, rather than basic ingredients. The most dramatic changes in expenditure behaviour have all taken place in luxury expenditure, including: recreational and cultural services, post and telecommunications, other goods and services (such as hairdressing, beauty counselling, etc.), and holidays. The British Tourist Authority estimate that overseas visitor spent £11.8 billion in 1995, of which 25% was spent shopping. It has been shown that towns and cities can benefit if they accommodate a diversity of activities to maintain their attractiveness (Figs. 4.26 and 4.27).

The only exception to this upward trend in expenditure relates to monetary services; in the 1990s this growth sector has slowed down significantly, particularly with the advent of direct line insurance and banking. Information technology, and its impact on productivity, is now reducing expenditure in this sector.

Fig. 4.26 (left). Towns and cities will prosper if they accommodate a diversity of activities; street theatre adds vitality.

Fig. 4.27 (right). The encouragement of street entertainment is an important ingredient to maintain the attractiveness of town and city centres.

The expenditure on recreation and cultural services is reflected in the growth of cinema attendances over the last decade (Table 4.10). It is estimated that total UK cinema admissions have increased from around 50 million in 1984 to over 120 million by 1994. It is not surprising that this trend has been reflected in the growth of multiplex cinema screens (Fig. 4.28). The Lakeside retail development in Thurrock, for example, not only includes a 1.1 million ft² shopping centre, but also over 2 million ft² of retail park uses, including multiplex cinemas. Figures have shown that more than 250 000 people visit the location per week and of these half buy a meal, which is not surprising as more than 40% of visitors are there for more than 3 hours and about 50% live at least

Table 4.10 Percentage of UK population who go to cinema

Year	%
1984	38
1986	53
1990	64
1992	62
1994	68

Source: Dodona Research.

Fig. 4.28. *The Point at Milton Keynes was the first multiplex cinema. Since it opened in the mid-1980s numbers have grown; there are now over 800 multiplex screens in Great Britain.*

Fig. 4.29. *The retail and leisure offer at The Wirral Leisure Park on Merseyside. The growth of car ownership has spawned a new type of urban land use.*

Fig. 4.30. *The renovation of the street cars in San Francisco, USA, has added to the attraction of the city as a leisure–retail location to be visited and revisited.*

Fig. 4.31. *South Street Sea Port, New York City, shows how life can be brought back to a city centre location.*

30 minutes' drive time from the development. The first freestanding multiplex screen, The Point, a pyramid-shaped building, in Milton Keynes, was developed in the mid-1980s. Since then the numbers have escalated and now account for more than one-third of all cinema screens in Great Britain, as shown in Table 4.11.

In 1996 the Richardson Brothers (creators of the Merry Hill Shopping Centre) proposed a 30-screen cinema complex for 6500 people at Spaghetti Junction outside Birmingham, on a 25-acre site to include restaurants, bars and shops. This is only one of a number of 30-screen complexes currently proposed by MCA and others. Since the Rank Leisure World complex at Hemel Hempstead, Hertfordshire, opened in 1995 on an 11-acre site it has attracted over 30 000 people each week. As with other such schemes, including the Wirral Leisure Park (Fig. 4.29) and the Finchley, North London, complex, such

Number	Multiplex screens	Other full-time	Total screens
1984	0	1126	1126
1985	10	1196	1206
1986	18	1168	1168
1987	42	1141	1183
1988	139	1174	1313
1989	285	1162	1447
1990	387	1162	1447
1991	510	1139	1649
1992	548	1131	1679
1993	606	1134	1740
1994	664	1126	1790
1995	702	1126 Est.	1828
1996	812 Est.	1126 Est.	1938

Table 4.11 Full-time cinema sites, screens and seats 1984–95

Source: Dodona Research and other.

	No. of sites	No. of screens
Virgin	19	143
Odeon	12	91
UCI	24	225
Showcase National Amusements	11	143
Warner	16	143

Table 4.12 Major UK multiplex companies 1996

Source: Various including Dodona, Richard Ellis and others.

developments combine cinemas with car parking, 10-pin bowling, bingo, nightclubs, restaurants and fast food outlets.

There is an expanding level of expertise including Warner Bros and Bass Leisure Entertainments, leasing such space. In late 1996 Virgin Cinemas stepped up its expansion programme by announcing plans for three giant cinemas ranging from 11 to 20 screens in South Shields, Bolton and Leeds, with the hope of creating 20 such multiplexes in the next 3 years. The major UK multiplex companies in 1996 are listed in Table 4.12.

The leisure industry and urban renewal

The leisure industry, and where people choose to spend leisure time, is one of the hopes for town and city centres in the twenty-first century. As *The Economist* stated on 6 July 1996:

Britain's cities have been brutally treated. In Manchester, Liverpool, Birmingham planners ripped out city centres and traditional streets and redesigned them with two ideas: the car and the zones ... Cars were given primacy, so that dual carriageways blasted a way along established neighbourhoods. As homes, factories, offices and shops were to be kept apart, so small shopping streets next to residential streets were destroyed in favour of lumping most retailers together in shopping malls.

In Britain, as in the United States of America, there have been attempts to bring back leisure uses and residents into city centres. *The Economist* suggests:

> The main reason for the flow of people back to the inner cities is their redevelopment. The government has bought this about largely by pouring money into some inner slums like Hulme in Manchester or old industrial waste lands like Docklands in London, where smart new estates welcome families and refurbished warehouses offer Manhattan-style lofts to young professionals.

In America there is talk of 'come back cities' (see, for example, Figs. 4.30–4.31). In places like Cleveland and Columbus in Ohio, as will be discussed in Chapter 6, cities have been turned inside out; the city centre has been turned into a destination for leisure activities. Over previous decades residents moved out, retailing moved out and employment moved out. What was left was a derelict land use vacuum, which has now been filled, as in down-town Atlanta, with leisure destination projects.

Fig. 4.32. Wigan Pier, Lancashire. The renovation by Wigan Borough Partnership of the area to include leisure uses as a result of the City Challenge Initiative, part of the Single Regeneration Budget.

Fig. 4.33. The Cheshire Oaks 'Designer' Outlet Village at Ellesmere Port, South Wirral near the junction of the M53 and M56. Its catchment covers Chester, North Wales, Birkenhead, Liverpool and Manchester.

Fig. 4.34. The Tracy Outlet Centre in northern California, USA has set a trend. It is close to an interstate highway interchange and hosts many international retail brand names.

To a greater or lesser degree, all towns and cities have an opportunity to recreate their urban environments, by bringing back leisure activities. The major question that has to be faced is: 'What do we mean by urban renewal?' There are numerous retail developments which have been constructed over the last decade which contribute to 'urban renewal'. One example is the renovation of Wigan Pier, Lancashire, by Wigan Borough Partnership (Fig. 4.32). Another example is the development of the Cheshire Oaks outlet retail centre near Ellesmere Port, on the edge of Merseyside (Fig. 4.33). This is similar to outlet centres in North America, such as the Tracy Outlet Centre in northern California (Fig. 4.34). Cheshire Oaks was opened in March 1995 and has 32 retail units with tenants like Jaegar, Bally and Nike. It is the biggest designer outlet centre in Europe, developed by BAA McArthur-Glen. Within months of opening the car park had overflowed and there was a shuttle bus to a neighbouring car park. Together with a new Sainsbury Hypermarket, Cheshire Oaks represent the renovation of a derelict urban area, being on the opposite side of the M53 motorway from the Ellesmere Port Oil Refinery.

Fig. 4.35. The new Alfred McAlpine Stadium, Huddersfield, UK. This development offers a whole range of commercial, sporting and entertainment opportunities. (Photograph: A.P.S. (UK))

Cheshire Oaks is a leisure-retail destination, but is likely to have an adverse impact (however small) on existing retail locations, which range from villages such as Eastham and Bromborough on the Wirral to larger retail locations like Birkenhead and Chester, all of which, and many more, are within 10–15 minutes' drive of this new scheme.

The growth of retail outlet centres represent the dynamic nature of retailing; PPG 6 will not prevent their continuing development. Unless traditional town and city centres reinvent themselves as locations for residential as well as leisure activities (for example, the new regional stadium at Huddersfield; Fig. 4.35) and have the political and financial power to implement such strategies (as will be discussed in Chapter 7), they are likely to continue to decline; retailers will only return to town centres if a combination of leisure and residential activities justify their presence.

CHAPTER 5

Cities: If not for work, then for what?

In recent decades there have been three distinct employment revolutions: the agricultural revolution, the manufacturing revolution and now the service sector revolution. Each of these employment sectors has, or is experiencing, major shifts in the quantity and type of employment. These trends will change the shape of the property market and the way we use town and city centres much faster than we expect.

The agricultural employment revolution
The increase in the productivity of the agriculture sector is demonstrated by the fact that, for a nation of 56 million people, with a working population of over 20 million, only about 250 000 people are directly employed in the agricultural sector. There has been a fall of almost 40% in those employed over the last 20 years; today, as can be seen in Table 5.1, only approximately 1% of all employment is in the agricultural industrial sector.

The twentieth-century agricultural employment revolution has taken place at a far greater speed than that of the eighteenth or nineteenth centuries, particularly on mainland Europe. A number of European countries had almost 20% of

Year	Total for GB	Employment in agriculture	Index	% GB
1975	22 213	388	100	1.81
1980	22 458	352	90	1.59
1985	20 572	321	82	1.54
1990	22 380	277	71	1.26
1995	21 522	250	64	1.18

Table 5.1 Agriculture employment trends ('000s)

Source: *Employment Gazette*, 1994 and *Labour Market Trends*, 1996.

Year	Employed in manufacturing	Index	%GB
1975	7351	100	34
1980	6801	92	31
1985	5254	71	25
1990	4994	67	22
1995	3840	52	20

Table 5.2 Manufacturing employment trend ('000s)

Source: *Employment Gazette*, 1994 and *Labour Market Trends*, 1996.

their employment in agriculture in the 1940s, which has now fallen to 5% or less. Great Britain, which led this employment trend, continues to be one of the most efficient in Europe in terms of both agricultural production and employment.

The manufacturing employment revolution

The revolution in employment productivity can also be seen in manufacturing (Table 5.2). In the last 20 years the number of employees involved with the manufacturing sector has fallen by 45%. In 1975 over 7 million people were directly employed in manufacturing industries, but the total has now fallen to less than 4 million. In many industries electronic robots have taken over the tasks of manual workers and are, for example, a major factor in car production, one of the largest sectors of manufacturing employment.

A similar trend can be seen for all production industries, namely those involved with both the manufacturing and the production of primary products such as coal, oil and energy. Here the total employment has fallen from around 8.5 million to 4.5 million with production employment now representing less than 22% of all employed in Great Britain. This improvement in manpower productivity has been partly stimulated by the privatization of utility companies.

The service sector employment revolution

The third employment revolution is now upon us; the service sector is going through a significant change brought about by a wide range of influences. Although it is widely suggested that the recent recession has been a service sector recession, this is not the case. Between 1990 and 1995 over 1.1 million jobs were lost in the manufacturing sector. In the same period over 500 000 jobs were created in the service sector of the economy (Table 5.3), but the jobs created were different from those in the booming 1980s.

Year	Employed in service	Index	%GB
1975	12 545	100	54
1980	13 384	107	58
1985	13 769	110	65
1990	15 609	124	68
1995	16 180	128	73

Table 5.3 Service employment trend ('000s)

Source: *Employment Gazette*, 1994 and *Labour Market Trends*, 1996.

Although in recent years there have been more than 2 million unemployed, the reality is that more than 90% of the employable workforce has been in employment. The service sector employment revolution is not creating massive levels of unemployment, but the nature of that employment is changing. In 1995, 75% of all employment was in the service sector, an increase from around 55% in 1975, 20 years earlier.

The myth of employment growth and the striving for productivity

Official statistics confirm trends from surveys of the office market, to be discussed later. The changing role of the service sector and the productivity of property is at the heart of the problem, and is linked to the myth surrounding employment and unemployment. The concept of the 'demographic timebomb' has been bandied about for many years but, as discussed in Chapter 2, it is only now that attention is beginning to be focused on the major financial problems which lie ahead. In the last four years the total workforce – that is those who could be gainfully employed - has fallen from almost 29 million to around 28 million. There have been fewer school leavers, more above retirement age and fewer able to claim unemployment money. In the last two years the total workforce in employment (in terms of full-time equivalent jobs) has remained relatively static at 25.9 million, having fallen by 1 million from the 1990 figure (Table 5.4). Unemployment has fallen for the major reason that those claiming unemployment benefit have decreased, not because the number of those in employment has significantly increased. The discussion regarding the appropriate methods of measuring these changes, perhaps using the Labour Forces Survey, continues.

The main reason, however, that the economy of Great Britain has been growing recently is borne out by other government figures which show that, although the workforce of Great Britain has fallen since 1990, the productivity (or output per person) has increased significantly, particularly in the manufacturing sector (Table 5.5).

In terms of employment and the use of office property, the squeeze will get worse; the service sector employment revolution has barely begun! Unlike the agricultural employment revolution and the manufacturing employment revolution, the service sector revolution may not be able to shed employment in aggregate. Many countries in Europe already have an unhealthy level of

Year	Employees	Workforce in employment	Total workforce
1990 December	22.7	26.9	28.8
1991 December	22.0	26.0	28.5
1992 December	21.5	25.4	28.4
1993 December	21.7	25.5	28.3
1994 December	21.8	25.7	28.2
1995 December	22.1	25.9	28.2
1996 June	22.2	25.9	28.0

Table 5.4 Employment: UK (millions)

Source: ONS, *Labour Market Trends*, December 1996.

	Workforce	Output per person employed
1990	100.3	100.5
1991	97.4	100.6
1992	95.2	102.0
1993	93.5	105.9
1994	94.0	109.7
1995	95.0	111.3
1996	95.2	113.5

Source: ONS, *Labour Market Trends*, December 1996.

Table 5.5 Workforce and output – quarter 2

unemployment and the political objective will be to keep as many people in employment as possible, although the pressures of the Maastricht Treaty, which are deflationary and inhibit employment, may prevail. However, those in certain types of employment in the future will have to be far more productive than in the past. This means that rather than reducing the overall level of employment, the service sector revolution will be far more concerned with the restructuring of employment to increase productivity. Smaller cost-efficient firms may prosper at the expense of larger firms, and property will also have to be far more cost-effective and productive. We will need fewer but more productive buildings, as well as a more productive workforce; and we will also need more productive urban areas, because inefficient urban areas in a competitive world will lose jobs.

The future sector trends

To understand the future, town planners and investors will increasingly distinguish between cyclical change (which is a relatively short-term phenomenon) and structural change (which is a medium- to long-term event). Table 5.6 sets out employment trends over the last 16 years, and the actual numbers employed in each government Standard Industrial Classifications, as at mid-1996. While recognizing the limitations of SIC codes, it does identify certain characteristics and point the way to future structural change. The table shows that there has been a steady decline in the number of people employed in the manufacturing sector. As previously discussed, employment has fallen by 32% since 1981. Partly as a result of privatization, there has been an even more dramatic drop in the number employed in the utility companies; since 1981 employment has fallen by 45%! Over the same time period the number employed in the service sector has increased by 25%, but only by 3% since the depth of the recession in 1990.

Within the service sector there are both winners and losers. Over the longer time period both retailing and the hotel/restaurant sectors have grown significantly; a growth of 13% and 38% respectively. Over the last five years there has been no continuing employment change growth in these sectors of the economy. Hotel chains such as Holiday Inn, Marriott, Hilton, Sheraton, Accor and Inter-Continental have international expansion plans. The London-based

World Travel and Tourism Council estimate that this industry now accounts for over 10% of world GDP.

Largely as a result of privatization and corporate change generally, transport/post office/telecommunications, together with public administration, have seen large falls in employment, falling by more than 11% since 1981; and both these sectors have seen employment fall during the 1990s. The financial intermediary sector (including retail and merchant banking) has shown significant employment growth over the longer time period; it has grown by 26% since 1981. However, during the 1990s it has seen a 5% fall in employment as technology has begun to replace job categories, particularly in retail banking. Direct line and cash point banking are here to stay.

A recent study by Douglas McWilliams at the Centre for Economic and Business Research for the London Chamber of Commerce and Industry was able to demonstrate that the financial sector, which accounts for 14.8% of London's GDP, is likely to grow by 14.3% to the year 2000. However, business services (33% of London's GDP) may grow by 20%. Although hotel and catering represents only 2.7% of London's GDP, it is forecast to grow by 27.2% by the year 2000.

Generally speaking the employment growth sectors are those areas of the economy which cannot be replaced by information technology. Hence, despite the fall in public administration employment, there has been a significant

	Mid-1996	Change since 1981	Change since 1990
Manufacturing	3.932	−22%	−15%
Utilities	0.203	−45%	−15%
Services	16.493	+25%	+3%
Within services			
Retailing	3.686	+13%	+2.4%
Hotels and restaurants	1.257	+38%	+3.4%
Transport/post/telecom	1.253	−11%	−9%
Financial intermediation	1.001	+26%	−5%
Business services (law/account/software/ real estate, computers, etc.)	2.805	+74%	+17%
Public administration	1.334	−11%	−4%
Education	1.764	+15%	−2%
Health activities	1.539	+23%	+6%
Social work	0.909	+76%	+14%

		Change since 1992
Part time: Male	1.323	+22%
Female	5.059	+5.3%
All	3.382	+7.7%
Self-employed persons (with or without employees)	3.199	−1.0%

Table 5.6 Employment trends: employees in employment in GB (millions)

Source: *Labour Market Trends*, December 1996.

	1979	1984	1990	1995/6
Full-time employees	76.7	69.7	67.1	65.2
Part-time employees	16.1	18.8	19.4	22.1
Full-time self-employed	6.5	9.4	11.3	10.2
Part-time self-employed	0.7	1.9	2.1	2.5

Table 5.7 The changing composition of employment percentages of all in employment

Source: Labour Force Survey.

growth over the last 15 years in employment in education, health activities, social work and other community activities, including entertainment (arts, leisure, sport, etc.). At the same time, business services nationally – including law, accountancy, software consultancy, management consultancy and real estate services – have overall shown a dramatic increase of 74% employment since 1981, and even a growth of 17% since 1990.

Forecasts from Oxford Economic Forecasting and others indicate that, in Great Britain, manufacturing employment will continue to fall, and 10 years from now far fewer will be employed in central and local government, in the utility companies and in financial services. Business services, including software consultancy, will expand still further, as will the hotel and restaurant sector. More will also be employed in social work, education and health.

Image of location (as will be discussed later), in an epoch of greater part-time employment, is increasingly important. In just three years from 1992 part-time employment increased by almost 8% and self-employment now accounts for about 13% of the workforce in employment (Table 5.7). This a continuation of a longer trend, as figures from 1979 onwards show. From an occupier's point of view, market forces of the future will dictate that the most efficient buildings, and the location of those buildings, will be those that reflect a low cost, high-quality work environment, in combination with a greater degree of flexibility.

It is often implied that this change in employment and the advance of technology will result in the death of the office building, and that we will all increasingly work at home. However, market evidence does not support this. Since 1991, when almost 27 million ft^2, or 15%, of the London office market was vacant, the vacancy level has fallen to below 10%; more than 9 million ft^2 has become occupied. Nevertheless, the role of the office is changing, and this has been influenced by international financial liberalization, the privatization of the public sector, corporate re-engineering in the private sector and the pressures for greater productivity. As Stuart Morley has observed, the Department of Environment's figures of office stock expanded 28% between 1984 and 1993, during which time the service sector employment growth was 15%. Now that the overall number of people working in office buildings is falling, this 'will mean that buildings from the 1970s (many of whose leases are near expiry) and earlier periods will be difficult to relet'.

The changing office market: privatization of the public sector
Official employment statistics are a reflection of major economic changes in recent years. The movement of global capital, for instance, is now becoming influential in the global property investment markets, particularly in Great

Britain. Relatively scarce global capital is looking for the highest rates of return, which is partly why real interest rates in Great Britain have recently been at an unusually high level. The Maastricht Treaty has further accelerated the pressure on financial markets within Europe to perform efficiently. Governments now have strict guidelines in terms of interest rates, currency stability, inflation and government spending. The globalization of the world financial markets, and of economies generally, has accelerated the need for manufacturing and service sector industries to become increasingly efficient.

What started as a political creed in the 1980s has now become a government financial imperative in many countries, regardless of whether the government is left or right of the political centre. The privatization of many public corporations has accelerated as governments have tried to both reduce their debt and make their industries more efficient, resulting in a major reassessment of employment needs and property requirements. And there is more to come: in his budget speech in November 1994, the Chancellor of Exchequer announced that he hoped to lay off an extra 24 000 civil servants over a period of five years. Assuming each employee occupies at least 100 ft^2, this shedding of staff alone represents around 2.5 million ft^2 of surplus accommodation to be disposed of by the government. In 1996 the Chancellor's budget speech projected a reduction of government expenditure by a further 7% over three years. The acceptance of the Private Finance Initiative will accelerate this process; the central government currently occupies around 5000 buildings, with about 118 million ft^2 of offices. This will contract to accommodate a shrinking quantity of floor space in the future.

As with the private sector, the public sector will seek office space productivity, which will not necessarily be delivered in town and city centres. It is estimated that, partly due to privatization, the number of public sector employees has already fallen from 730 000 in 1979 to around 500 000 in 1996. In 1996 Birmingham Council, for instance, announced it would introduce high-tech working methods among its 40 000 employees in an attempt to cut spending on office space; this is yet more evidence of a trend to downsize office employment in the public sector.

Re-engineering of the private sector

The word 're-engineering' has become a buzz word to sum up the pressure changing the structure of private corporations and service sector employment generally. It started during the recession in North America in the late 1980s and has now become endemic in all mature economies.

A survey of 480 office occupiers in Great Britain during 1994 (conducted by The Harris Research Centre commissioned by Richard Ellis), found that 56% of companies interviewed expected the structure of their industry to change over the next five years (Table 5.8), with 30% expecting their own particular company to be restructured (Table 5.9); 31% also believed that their own company would be involved with a merger or takeover within this five-year period (Table 5.10). The survey also found that 32% of companies were already involved with, or were considering, 'outsourcing' an element of production or some of their services, as a way to make them more competitive (Table 5.11). This trend is confirmed by the CBI Quarterly Industrial Trends Survey which

Major changes	30%
Minor changes	26%
No changes	41%
Don't know	3%

Source: Richard Ellis.

Table 5.8 Whether their industry structure will change

Yes	30%
No	66%
Don't know	4%

Source: Richard Ellis.

Table 5.9 Plans for company restructure within the next 5 years

Likely	31%
Not very likely	61%
Don't know	9%

Source: Richard Ellis.

Table 5.10 Likelihood of company merger/takeover over next 5 years

Currently have a strategy	13%
Considering developing a strategy	19%
No plans to 'outsource'	66%
Don't know	2%

Source: Richard Ellis.

Table 5.11 Whether company is 'outsourcing'

reveals that, since a low ebb in 1991, companies employing less than 200 staff have generally prospered far better than firms employing over 500. The output of larger firms has improved, but it has not resulted in the overall growth of employment; smaller firms have generally been taking on labour.

In connection with this trend towards productivity, more than a third of companies interviewed for Richard Ellis admitted that 10% or more of their staff were already involved with 'hot desking', whereby a number of employees share the same work space and visit their office building on an occasional basis. This trend is confirmed by government figures which show that part-time employment has increased by 25% in the last decade, with over 80% of almost 6 million part-time workers now being female. In 1996 it was estimated that almost all the full-time equivalent jobs created since the recession in 1990/91 had been part time; the work space requirements for this type of workforce will be very different to office buildings of the past.

Re-engineering and property location

Overall it was not surprising that 31% of all companies interviewed by the Harris Research Centre for Richard Ellis believed that they would be relocating their premises over the next five years. The factors influencing relocation are to some extent a reflection of the drive towards greater productivity. This is also reflected in the Black Horse Relocation Survey which indicated that happy and skilled staff reduce the motivation to move, as shown in Tables 5.12 and 5.13. The same survey (Table 5.14) identified the skills which a quality workforce

(527 respondents = 71% of total sample)

Happy with current location, no need to move	26%
Experienced/skilled staff at current location	11%
Too costly to move/benefit wouldn't cover cost	11%
Establish a long time/strong business roots	9%
Room for expansion/new development at current location	6%
Don't wish to lose established customer base	6%
Recent development of current site	6%
Only recently moved to current location	4%

Table 5.12 Main reasons why unlikely to relocate

Source: Black Horse Relocation Services Ltd.

(151 respondents = 20% of total sample)

Need to expand company	34%
No space left at current site	14%
To reduce costs/overheads	8%
Currently looking for new site	7%
Present site unsatisfactory	7%

Table 5.13 Main reasons why likely to relocate

Source: Black Horse Relocation Services Ltd.

Foreign language skills	2%
Management skills	17%
Computer literacy/IT ability	22%
Customer care skills	28%
Communication skills	31%
Ability to work well with others	36%
Basic level of skill to build on	36%
Job specific skills	37%
Basic numeracy and literacy	41%
Team working skills	47%

Table 5.14 Importance of work skills

Percentages: Multiple response possible.
Base: All respondents (742)
Source: Black Horse Relocation Services Ltd.

would need to possess; skilled staff able to work in teams dominate the findings.

As Ian Angell, Professor of Information Systems at LSE, stated recently:

> Companies are globalizing and mobilizing, chasing 'spot markets' in cyberspace. The cost of over coming time and space no longer buffer the impact of cheap labour. The state has to be part of the global economy.

This is reflected in the growth of call-centres, those offices buildings specializing in telephone direct marketing by banking, airline, insurance, charities and many other markets. The Henley Centre for Forecasting estimates more than 2 million people will be employed world wide in telemarketing by the end of the decade; India, USA and many other countries now compete with Great Britain for this type of employment. Three years ago there were no call-centres in Ireland; in 1996 there were 42 foreign and domestic companies, a figure likely to double by the year 2000. Other cities such as Leeds (Fig. 5.1), Cardiff (Fig. 5.2) and Sheffield have seen employment growth in this sector. Although many

Fig. 5.1. Princes Square, Leeds. A 106 000 ft² development adjacent to Leeds railway station by Teesland Development Co. (Northern) Limited and Railtrack Property. Workspace in Yorkshire for the next millennium, located on top of a public transport interchange facility.

99

Fig. 5.2. An aerial view of Cardiff Bay, a major urban regeneration project where the Development Corporation and the local planning authorities are co-operating to change the face of south Cardiff, including attracting call-centre tenants. (Photograph: Grosvenor Waterside.)

call-centre office buildings are on the edge of town or are out-of-town centres, some cities, like Glasgow claiming to be the capital of call-centres, have targeted this market. Employees work a typical part-time shift of 4–6 hours but do not necessarily need to work in Great Britain. The emphasis is on work skills, using information technology, reducing costs and increasing productivity by employing part-time staff.

Table 5.15 illustrates typical office occupation costs for three locations in Great Britain. It shows the very low cost of fuel (normally gas) and electricity relative to other costs, excluding labour. But occupation costs normally only reflect about 5% of the annual turnover of an office occupier yet labour costs represent more than 50% and have a major impact on employment location decisions. If it is assumed that an employee occupies 100 ft^2 (10 m^2), office occupation costs are likely to be in the region of £3000 per year, yet the salary and pension costs are likely to be between 5 and 10 times this sum. The productivity of the salary (person employed) is far more important than the office occupation cost; in other words, the productivity of a building is largely related to those who work within the building, which is why the design and location of office buildings (Fig. 5.3) and the role of facilities managers are becoming increasingly important.

The three most important factors influencing relocation, identified by the Harris Research/Richard Ellis Survey, were: the occupational cost of the building, the quality of buildings available and the road infrastructure. If the quality of the building and road accessibility to the building do not encourage employee productivity, it will not be favoured. Table 5.16 shows that of 17 possible factors, the need for a city centre location was placed last! City centres

	West End of London	Regional capital	Thames London
Fuel	£1.70	£0.60	£0.65
Decorations	£0.10	£0.10	£0.30
M & E (head, airconditioning, lifts)	£1.15	£0.50	£0.85
Cleaning	£0.60	£0.50	£0.80
Building services	£0.15	£0.30	£0.20
Building management	£0.50	£0.00	£0.75
Security	£1.70	£0.35	£0.00
Management fees	£0.60	£0.50	£0.25
Sub totals	£6.50	£2.85	£4.10
Insurance	£1.35	£0.95	£0.95
Total service charge	£7.85	£3.80	£5.05
Rates, say	£10.00	£5.00	£8.00
Rent, say	£30.00	£15.00	£20.00
Total occupation cost	£47.85	£23.80	£33.05

Table 5.15 Office occupation cost data in 1996 (per ft²)

Source: Richard Ellis.

overall now appear to be regarded as unproductive and expensive in the age of the third employment revolution, the service sector revolution.

Leyla Boulton and Gillian Tett stated in the *Financial Times* of 5 August 1996 that a recent Confederation of British Industry study suggested that traffic congestion, delaying the movement of goods and staff, added £15 billion a year to business costs. This is a cost which makes British towns and cities less competitive in a competing global market place.

Office location, planning policy and transport infrastructure
The government has no specific guidance towards an integrated national office and transport policy. However, there are a number of initiatives which will have an impact on the office market. Firstly, in common with European directives, the government will increase the level of taxation on motor fuel, at a rate which is faster than inflation, as a means of raising revenue, controlling air pollution and reducing dependence on road travel. The Government Green Paper *Transport: The Way Forward* in April 1996 demonstrated an awareness of this problem. Secondly, the revised *Planning Policy Guidance Note 6*, released during the Summer of 1996, follows on from the earlier PPG 6 and PPG 13 which placed an 'emphasis on the importance of a coherent town centre parking strategy in maintaining urban vitality, through a combination of location, management and pricing of parking for different user groups'.

The implication of trends in the market, however, is that those better locations which already have good accessibility, together with good car-parking facilities, are likely to become more valuable. Planning policy is unlikely to significantly reduce the growth, popularity or productivity of out-of-town office development as the preferred location for many office employers. Planning policy is also unlikely to have an impact on the problems of road speeds (Table 5.17) or congestion.

What has been extraordinary about the office town planning policies of the last 50 years is the lack of understanding of the impact that the growth of road technology and car ownership has had on office locations. There have often been restrictions on car parking associated with office development in town centres, yet little has been invested in good public transport to compensate for these restrictions and out-of-town office development has consequently mush-roomed.

The dilemma most urban planners have is rarely articulated clearly. One of the responses to clarifying urban policy was put to the author in 1994 with the following:

The approach in Leeds (UK) towards town planning differentiates between short-stay and long-stay parking. Long-stay commuter trips create morning and evening peaks of road usage. An important priority for the Leeds Transport Strategy and the Leeds UDP is to seek to reduce the problems of peak hour congestion, whilst acknowledging that car travel remains the preference for many commuters. Therefore, a balanced

Fig. 5.3. The award-winning NCM building, developed by Grosvenor Waterside, overlooking the inner harbour at Cardiff Bay, rejuvenating an urban area with a top quality work environment. (Photograph: Grosvenor Waterside Plc, a subsidiary of Associated British Ports Holdings Plc.)

1 = no influence at all; 10 = a great deal of influence	
	Average score by interviewees
Total building occupational costs	8.08
Quality of buildings	7.65
Road infrastructure	7.61
Security of the area	7.50
Availability of staff in the area	7.39
Availability of car parking	7.22
Quality of life for employees	6.88
Access to the client/target market	6.57
Qualification/skills of staff in the area	6.15
Out of city centre/edge of town	5.74
Prestige location	5.01
Spouse's employment prospects in the area	4.59
Rail infrastructure	4.54
Air infrastructure	4.07
Competing companies in the area	3.96
Availability of part-time staff in the area	3.88
City centre location	3.40

Source: Richard Ellis.

Table 5.16 Factors influencing the search for new premises

	m.p.h.
Peterborough	36.8
Teeside	31.6
Swindon	26.8
Plymouth	25.2
Bournemouth/Poole	23.3
Brighton/Hove	23.2
Coventry	22.1
Tyneside	21.8
Grimsby/Cleethorpes	21.8
Oxford	20.3
Leeds/Bradford	19.6
Merseyside	18.5
West Midlands	18.3
Bristol	18.0
Norwich	18.0
Greater Manchester	17.4
Sheffield	17.1
Leicester	15.8
London	8.0

Source: Department of Transport, 1994.

Table 5.17 Road commuting speeds in Great Britain

strategy has been adopted which seeks to control the growth of car-borne commuting to this city centre. Long-stay parking provision will be used as a strategic tool to elevate peak hour congestion and reduce environmental conflicts.

The growth of long-stay commuter car parking related to city centre employment will be managed as follows:

1. Parking provision on new developments should reflect the city council's long-stay commuter parking guidelines which distinguish between:

    - within and immediately adjoining the public transport box, where additional parking will be discouraged;
    - the city centre core, where the provision of additional commuter parking will be restrained; and
    - fringe city centre areas, where the objective is to control the growth the commuter parking by adopting differential standards between defined zones.

2. Further on-street parking restrictions will be introduced, accompanied by schemes giving priority to residents parking and the needs of local firms in the defined fringe area.

3. Support will be given to park and ride schemes involving metropolitan, supertram or bus services in accordance with policy.

The reply from the Leeds City Council suggests:

the long-stay parking guidelines generally become more relaxed in rings away from the core reflecting poorer accessibility by public transport, the need to recognise on-street parking problems and the types of use to be found. Within the public transport box, and to a lesser extent the city centre core, the key objectives are to reduce extraneous through traffic, increase pedestrianisation, improve the environment and minimise the vehicular-pedestrian conflict.

The policies cited by Leeds City Council are repeated in other cities. For instance the planning department of the City of Glasgow says:

the future supply of public car parking should support the integrated strategy by encouraging public transport usage, effective restraint of private car commuting and ensure that parking is available only to shoppers and business visitors on a short-stay basis and that supply should continue to be tested against these criteria.

Birmingham City Council (UK) says that their car parking policy has been to:

maximize the net revenue from car parking consistent with the implementation of planning, development and transport policies. These objectives reflect the importance of the City Councils controlled car parking as a revenue generator; the City Councils perception that the city centre is of critical importance to the economic, social and environmental well being of the city; and the role of public transport in meeting troubled demand. The overall policy position of the City Council represents a trade-off between these considerations.

In the examples of Leeds, Glasgow and Birmingham the role of car parking is generally seen as a problem which needs to be controlled in the city centre, rather than a positive asset to make businesses prosper. Throughout the Western world physical town planners do not seem to have realized what has happened in terms of the creation of either out-of-town business parks or the expansion of office development in towns where accessibility and car parking is made easier than in the traditional business districts of major metropolitan areas. A radical shift in thinking, and a complete U-turn in policy, is needed if cities are to survive as business wealth generators.

When IBM chose North Harbour, Portsmouth, on the M27 motorway as a site for their major European office buildings, Hampshire County Council realized in the early 1980s that over 70% of IBM's employees travelled to the facility by car and that similar sites should be found within Hampshire. The Solent Business Park appeared a few year later. This was a rare example of strategic town planning but it did little to assist existing town centre office locations.

Imagine what may have evolved if town planning policy had been radically different; if each office building constructed over the last few decades had been permitted to provide car parking for at least 70% of occupants. Imagine that there had been a specific office car-parking tax, over and beyond business rates, which had been deliberatively reinvested in the public transport bus, tram and rail network. The problems of urban office dereliction which exist today might have been avoided. Surplus office buildings would be much easier to adapt to alternative uses in an era of shrinking office demand.

What economists call 'the elasticity of demand' for car usage is extremely high relative to public transport. The convenience of travelling by car is so strong that raising the cost of travel (for instance by taxing fuel) has a very small impact on car usage. Put simply, a journey by car (even allowing for congestion) which takes over an hour may be equivalent to a journey by public transport taking only 45 minutes, particularly if 10 minutes of this time involves waiting for a bus or train in the cold and wet, and not being sure that the bus or train will arrive uncrowded or on time.

With reference to the changing nature of demand, a good-quality transport infrastructure will be vital to the future investment performance of office markets. It is insufficient to measure transport infrastructure simply in terms of road transport, rail transport or air transport, for both in-town and out-of-town office buildings. The key will be the quality and convenience of any particular mode of transport to and from those locations which are perceived as attractive to the shrinking quantity of office employment. In other words, for example, even if there appears to be insufficient car parking at Canary Wharf (Fig. 5.4), if the rail transport to Canary Wharf improves significantly, then this area will

Fig. 5.4. The tower at Canary Wharf in London's Docklands. A business location for the international meritocratic élite of the twenty-first century.

be perceived as a desirable location to work for the meritocratic élite and the investment worth of Canary Wharf will rise significantly.

Ironically, in the case of a development on the west side of London recently, the town planners insisted on a dramatic increase in car-parking provision. However, as the site had access to the London Underground railway and the M25 motorway, the occupier market did not justify such a high car-parking standard. By contrast, simply improving the transport infrastructure, for instance, into the heart of other older industrial cities may be insufficient; the heart of some cities are unlikely, in the short term, to be an attractive environment to knowledge-based 'intellectual property' styles of employment of the future; they are not the natural home for the meritocratic élite to work in the late twentieth century.

The next millennium

So far this chapter has discussed changing employment patterns, evidence from surveys of office occupiers and planning policy, particularly with reference to transport issues. However, the major influence on the change in employment patterns is summed up by Professor Jeremy Rifkin in his book *The End of Work*: 'We are moving into the information age; computers and robots are replacing whole job categories.' This theme was picked up by the symposium in

Disneyland in Paris in 1995 entitled *The City in 2020*. Increasingly the most important workspace (office buildings) will be created for those involved with knowledge-based jobs or 'intellectual property'. The continuing rise of the meritocratic élite will dominate the value of the best office investments.

As the drift continues away from the strictly repetitive tasks (which will be undertaken by computers) towards the need for greater individual skills, together with collaborative team work, building design will need to change to cope with the greater degree of flexibility in this new culture. The Paris symposium suggested that new forms of workplace will be housed in flexible, multi-function buildings – a trend that can be seen at Brindleyplace, Birmingham (Fig. 5.5).

These themes are already apparent from employment change; as mentioned earlier, since 1981 the number of people employed in the computer sector of the economy has increased by 66%, and even in the last five years employment has continued to increase by 12%. Many of these employees, however, are very location specific; the Thames Valley, West of London, for instance, has become one of the most popular locations. But such towns as Oxford, Cambridge, Guildford and Bath also have problems associated with being too popular. Whenever a town creates a park-and-ride transport network, it is a clear sign of the positive polarization of geographic land uses. Inner city office buildings remain unlet yet university towns, with an acceptable image, attract the meritocratic élite, even though the educational quality of the workforce in cities like Sheffield or Newcastle may be of equal or perhaps superior calibre. To enable office occupiers to attract the best knowledge-based employees, office buildings will have to be located in those areas of the country in which employees wish to live. The implication, as mentioned earlier, is that for good

Fig. 5.5 The Central Square at Brindleyplace, Birmingham. The rejuvenation of a city centre location for the meritocratic élite of the twenty-first century. Tenants so far include Lloyds Bank and BT on a 17-acre mixed-use site involving offices, restaurants, bars, shops, canal side homes and leisure facilities. (Photograph: Brindleyplace Plc/Simon Hazelgrove Photography.)

or for bad the popularity of the Thames Valley (and west M25 generally; Figs 5.6 and 5.7) will continue to attract major international office occupiers.

Another implication of this trend is that the Thames Gateway initiative, to boost employment on the east side of London, is likely to have a limited success and the investment performance of office buildings in this area of southern England will be mediocre. The Millennium project on the Greenwich Peninsular (which has similarities with the EuroDisney project on the less favoured east side of Paris) may provide a stimulus to an alternative employment structure.

The recent announcement that Norwich proposed a Technopolis (similar to the French concept of Techno Pols) fits the challenge for office employment in the future. Although Colin Amery (*Financial Times*, 22 April 1996) said, 'Have the city of Norwich and the county of Norfolk gone completely mad?' and that it is '... so far removed from reality as to be virtually out of sight', there is much sense in the madness.

A short distance across East Anglia the Cambridge phenomenon goes from strength to strength. The Cambridge Science Park, a site of 130 acres owned by Trinity College and the St John's College Innovation Centre, points the way ahead and has created a large number of jobs. The Surrey Science Research

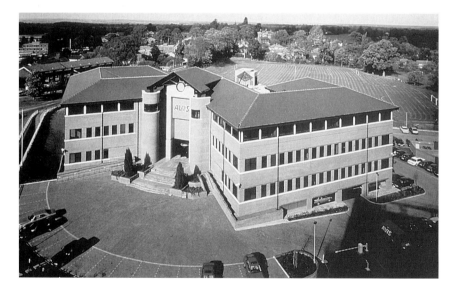

Fig. 5.6. Park Gate, Bracknell. The interior showing the central atrium, a sense of place to attract the better staff. (Photograph: Damond Lock Grabowski & Partners.)

Fig. 5.7. Park Gate, Bracknell. An office building developed in the growth western side of London; an out-of-town scheme providing flexibility in use, let to Avis. (Photograph: Damond Lock Grabowski & Partners.)

Fig. 5.8. The Surrey Science Research Park. A joint venture involving the University of Surrey, providing a landscaped setting to attract business space for the scientific meritocratic élite of the late twentieth century.

Fig. 5.9. Stockley Park, West London. One of the most successful business parks created in the last decade for the meritocratic élite.

Park and Stockley Park, west London (Figs 5.8 and 5.9) are also having an impact on regional employment.

The Black Horse survey of business ranked 48 UK cities in terms of where people would like to work (Table 5.18). The top 10 provides an interesting insight into future business trends. What is worrying is the number of significant business locations missing from the top 10, including London, Glasgow, Southampton, Leicester and Liverpool.

Increasingly, office employment will be limited to a shrinking workforce; it will be influenced by the meritocratic élite. Where they prefer to live and work will determine the most valuable office buildings in the future. Town and city centres have a choice; to struggle to seek ways to attract this employment or adapt and change and follow a different strategy. By encouraging mixed residential development and leisure industry uses (one of the employment

Rank 1996	Rank 1995	City
1 =	1 =	Oxford
1 =	5	Edinburgh
3	1 =	Bristol
4 =	3 =	Cambridge
4 =	6	Manchester
6	3 =	Birmingham
7 =	15 =	Newcastle upon Tyne
7 =	10 =	Nottingham
7 =	7 =	Leeds
10 =	10 =	Plymouth
10 =	7 =	Exeter

Table 5.18 Most desirable UK cities for relocation

Source: Black Horse Relocation Services Ltd.

growth sectors of the present and future) they will survive and perhaps prosper. Indirectly they may attract office employment; however, many town and city centres need to wake up to the reality of structural change and harness this energy to their benefit.

Offices: the investment market delusion

Employment changes in the service sector have been increasingly reflected in the performance of offices, as an investment class, since 1980. Firstly, clear cyclical patterns are to be detected in the performance of the market; but, secondly, and more worrying, structural changes are taking place which the market (both investors and town planners) has neither fully anticipated nor understood. I have set out in Table 5.19 the total performance of the office market (rental income received plus capital growth) against the total returns from equities and gilts.

Using both the Richard Ellis Monthly Index and IPD figures shows that direct office investment total returns only out performed equities and gilts in 1987 and 1988; all other years since 1980 have produced underperformance. Although the volatility is lower (the standard deviation) the total performance over the longer term has also been worse for offices, compared with equities and gilts.

| Year | Total returns | | | |
| | Offices | | Gilts | Equities |
	REMI	IPD		
1980	25.7	16.4	21.1	35.0
1981	18.8	14.9	1.4	13.5
1982	12.9	6.6	53.9	28.9
1983	9.7	5.3	16.2	28.8
1984	7.1	6.3	7.3	31.6
1985	6.0	7.3	11.3	20.6
1986	3.7	11.5	11.7	27.5
1987	20.9	29.6	16.3	8.0
1988	36.0	30.2	9.4	11.6
1989	19.6	15.9	5.7	36.0
1990	−11.6	−9.6	4.2	−9.7
1991	−13.2	−10.6	18.6	20.7
1992	−1.7	−6.8	17.0	20.4
1993	20.8	18.5	34.4	28.4
1993	12.1	10.6	−12.2	−5.8
1995	1.9	2.8	16.4	23.9
Average	9.8	8.7	13.7	19.2
Standard deviation	12.8	11.6	14.1	13.0

Table 5.19 Total investment returns (income received plus capital change)

Source: Investment Property Databank and Richard Ellis Monthly Index.

Office performance relative to other sectors

Offices have also performed badly compared with other property sectors. I have set out in Table 5.20 the performance of offices, compared with the total return received from the retail sector and the industrial sector over a number of years. This clearly shows that the office market performance has been more volatile (ranging from over 20% in 1987 to minus 10% or worse in both 1990 and 1991) than the other sectors (apart from industrials) but has also clearly under-performed in terms of the average annual performance of all the other sectors.

What is also often not appreciated is that office buildings in London and southern England, particularly suburban London, have not performed particularly well as investments compared with the rest of UK. Table 5.21 shows that, even in the good years, London offices were not significantly better than the rest of UK, which did not suffer as badly in the recession years of 1990 to 1992. Overall Great Britain has constructed too many office buildings, many of which are nowadays of poor quality and redundant.

The problems of the office sector are summed up by suburban London. Table 5.22 shows that the average rental growth over 14 years was only 1.4% in nominal terms – a long way behind average inflation of 6.3%. Suburban London suffers from a poor stock of offices, extreme road congestion, poor public transport in parts and a below calibre workforce in some districts. It is the dead doughnut ring of the office market with the core of London still able to attract the best and the M25 towns, particularly on the west, also able to attract the meritocratic élite.

Year	Office		Retail		Industrial		Retail warehouse
	REMI	IPD	REMI	IPD	REMI	IPD	REMI
1980	25.7	16.4	22.7	18.9	16.8	16.7	–
1981	18.8	14.9	18.1	17.1	15.9	12.2	18.6
1982	12.9	6.6	9.7	10.2	10.7	5.7	7.7
1984	7.1	6.3	16.7	13.5	5.0	6.0	19.7
1985	6.0	7.3	13.1	12.3	3.5	3.4	20.7
1986	3.7	11.5	13.1	11.4	9.1	8.6	12.8
1987	20.9	29.6	21.2	20.1	30.2	23.3	15.2
1988	36	30.2	24.2	23.8	51.9	37.1	37.9
1989	19.6	15.9	5.8	9.8	28.8	28.3	9.1
1990	−11.6	−9.6	−7.7	−8.1	−1.3	−3.6	−5.7
1991	−13.2	−10.6	6.7	2.9	12.9	8.4	15.0
1992	−1.7	−6.8	0.8	3.2	8.5	0.9	21.5
1993	20.7	18.5	19.9	19.8	20.7	19.6	30.3
1994	12.1	10.6	11.2	12.8	15.7	11.2	21.0
1995	1.9	2.8	1.4	3.4	−2.8	2.7	4.5
Average	9.8	8.7	11.8	11.2	13.2	11.2	15.2
Standard deviation	12.8	11.6	8.6	7.8	13.9	10.5	10.4

Table 5.20 Total returns from property sectors

Source: Investment Property Databank and Richard Ellis Monthly Index.

	Central London	Rest of London	Southern England	Rest of UK
1985	10.4	0.9	5.0	4.8
1986	18.1	2.7	1.4	3.5
1987	38.5	20.3	13.1	14.9
1988	30.3	36.0	26.9	28.7
1989	12.6	18.1	19.8	34.0
1990	−11.8	−7.2	−9.3	1.1
1991	−17.6	−5.7	−3.0	5.2
1992	−9.5	−8.2	−4.5	1.9
1993	19.5	15.1	17.2	18.4
1994	12.0	6.5	8.1	11.5
1995	4.7	−0.9	1.3	1.1
1985–95	8.3	6.8	6.5	11.5
1990–95	0.9	1.0	3.5	7.4

Table 5.21 The office market: total annual returns London and the UK

Source: IPD Property Investors Digest 1996.

Within the South East Region figure there are major variations. The geographic bias of the office market is further illustrated by the Richard Ellis survey of the M25 office market (Figs 5.6–5.9). Measuring all occupied offices over 5000 ft^2 in a corridor 8 miles in and 12 miles out from the motorway shows that the vast majority of take-up has been on the west side where the meritocractic élite wish to live. In the five years to the end of 1996, 12.94 million ft^2 of offices became occupied in the western quadrant, compared with 6.10 million ft^2 in the north, 5.21 million ft^2 in the south, and only 1.46 million ft^2 in the eastern quadrant.

As discussed in Chapter 2, the 'hot spot' in terms of M25 office activity is also a 'hot spot' for residential development. Office employers, seeking the most able and productive employees in southern England outside central

Office regions	% Growth
Suburban London	1.4
South East	2.3
South West	5.8
East Anglia	4.7
East Midlands	6.6
West Midlands	7.0
Wales	4.3
North West	6.2
North	5.3
Yorkshire and Humberside	5.9
Scotland	6.0
Inflation	6.3

Table 5.22 Historic rental percentage growth 1980–94

Source: Investment Property Databank.

	Standard offices	Office parks
1985	7.3	9.0
1986	11.5	7.8
1987	29.7	19.6
1988	30.3	23.0
1989	15.9	18.1
1990	–9.7	–9.3
1991	–11.1	2.7
1992	–6.8	–6.3
1993	18.5	18.7
1994	10.4	12.7
1995	2.8	3.7
1985–95	8.2	8.5
1990–95	2.2	6.0

Table 5.23 The office market: Year-on-year total returns (%)

Source: IPD *Property Investor's Digest*, 1996.

London, increasingly gravitate to where their employees want to live. There is also evidence that the office workforce of the 1990s prefers out-of-town campus style office parks (Table 5.23), often providing good road accessibility and good car parking. Office park rents did not fall as dramatically in the early 1990s, since when rents have grown slightly faster reflecting stronger market demand, which is reflected in investment returns.

The pricing of office market investment assets

The investment market and town planners have been slow to realize, not only the strong geographic bias of the market but the generally poor performance of offices. Table 5.24 presents an assessment of both the actual market yield and the 'implied' yield at which offices should have been trading at different points in time since 1977. To assess the 'implied' office market yield I have taken, as our benchmark, the income return on long-dated government gilts at a given moment in time, plus 3%. This in effect is regarded as the target Internal Rate of Return. Against this target I have then calculated average rental growth over a future five-year period and, for the purposes of this analysis, have assumed that this rental growth is indefinite. From 1991 onwards we have input forecast rental growth figures.

Based upon these two assumptions, I have then calculated the office yield which should have been paid for an average portfolio of office investments at a given moment in time, to meet these two criteria (the Internal Rate of Return and the expected rental growth). The 'implied' yield, as you can see, increased significantly at the end of the 1980s. It is only recently that the 'implied' office investment yield has come back to the yield being paid in the marketplace.

The overall conclusion is that office assets were briefly underpriced by the market during the early 1980s (between 1983 and 1985) but considerably overpriced at the end of the 1980s (from 1986 until 1992); the market did not anticipate the depth of the recession to come. During the boom years investors on average paid prices that were much too high, but they also failed to

Year End	'Implied' yield on offices (Gilt yield + 3%)	Average equivalent yield on UK offices
1977	4.83	6.80
1978	8.52	6.80
1979	11.57	5.73
1980	12.60	5.69
1981	15.25	5.87
1982	7.68	5.26
1983	2.48	5.56
1984	−0.45	7.02
1985	0.20	7.47
1986	6.95	6.54
1987	12.95	7.36
1988	17.73	6.90
1989	19.28	6.57
1990	19.77	8.66
1991	16.12	8.95
1992	10.61	8.92
1993	4.14	7.01
1994	6.33	6.60
1995	5.80	7.50

Table 5.24 Office investment yield analysis

Source: Richard Ellis Monthly Index and other sources.
NB: Wherever the average equivalent yield is lower than the 'implied yield', the market is overvaluing office investments.

understand how the office employment market was structurally changing. Great Britain overall has created a surplus of poor-quality office buildings, producing an unsatisfactory investment performance, despite some better designed and better located buildings producing good investment returns.

Office market returns: income vs capital

Office investments became most popular in the growth years of the 1970s. Table 5.25 shows the proportions of returns from the office market, over a period of years, which can be attributable to either rental income received or capital change. The table clearly indicates that during periods of high inflation in the early and late 1970s, capital growth was a significant component of the office total return capital growth. In recent years the majority of all total returns has been received from income, not capital change. This trend is likely to continue in an era of low inflation and relatively modest rental growth which, in turn, will have only a modest impact on capital growth. Capital change, caused by a significant downward movement in office investment yields, is also unlikely in the future.

Year	Office total returns	Office income return	Office capital growth
1971	18.8	4.6	14.2
1972	32.7	4.4	28.3
1973	30.2	3.9	26.2
1974	−18.4	3.6	−22.0
1975	7.8	5.5	2.4
1976	6.9	5.7	1.2
1977	22.7	6.3	16.4
1978	22.1	5.7	16.4
1979	19.9	5.5	14.3
1980	16.4	5.5	10.9
1981	14.9	5.4	9.4
1982	6.6	5.3	1.3
1983	5.3	5.6	−0.3
1984	6.3	5.9	0.4
1985	7.3	6.2	1.2
1986	11.5	6.4	5.1
1987	29.6	6.5	23.1
1988	30.2	5.9	24.4
1989	15.9	5.4	10.5
1990	−9.6	5.4	−15.1
1991	−10.6	6.8	−17.4
1992	−6.8	8.2	−15.0
1993	18.5	9.4	9.1
1994	10.6	8.3	2.3
1995	2.8	7.8	−5.0
Average	10.9	6.0	4.8
Standard deviation	13.1	1.3	13.4

Table 5.25 Office investment returns dis-aggregated

Source: Richard Ellis Monthly Index and other sources.

Investors (including bankers providing investment finance) and town planners (as will be discussed in greater detail in Chapter 7) are now beginning to realize the office market is no longer, and may never be, a crock of gold to be plundered in the future for capital growth to create an investment return or to pay for planning gains.

CHAPTER 6

The future of cities in an epoch of growing global competition

Will Shanghai in China, already having a population of more than 8 million, be the financial capital of the world by the middle of the next century (Fig. 6.1)? All the ingredients are now in place; it is also one of China's largest cities with an historic base as a commercial and financial centre in a country of more than 1.2 billion people. In recent years China has had over 10% economic growth, industrial production increased by 14% p.a., inflation has been below 10% and both the trade and current account balances have been well into surplus. China's foreign currency reserves almost doubled in recent years and are now higher than those in Singapore. China's clear aim is to create a world class centre based at Pudong on the east side of the Huangpu River, outside the traditional Paxi centre of Shanghai; 100 square kilometres may have been developed by the year 2000.

In the same way that New York is arguably the financial capital of America, and Washington the political centre, Shanghai may develop as a financial city while Beijing will remain the political capital in China, but will Beijing be the political capital of the world in the twenty-first century? The role of Hong Kong remains uncertain; from 1997 onwards Hong Kong will seek to find a new position in the new world order, increasingly dominated by mainland China. But the uncertainties over Hong Kong are reflected to some extent in the continuing success of Singapore, a city which has shown remarkable growth over the last half century, where per capita income is now higher than in Great Britain and where rental values for office buildings have continued to rise in contrast to the pattern of rental growth and political uncertainty of Hong Kong. In both Hong Kong and Tokyo rents fell during the mid-1990s, reflecting the economic and political uncertainties of these two cities.

Tokyo is one of the most expensive cities, not only in Asia but in the world to occupy office space, but one has to question whether the future of rental

Fig. 6.1. The Bund, Shanghai, China. Will Shanghai be the financial capital of the world in the twenty-first century? (Photograph: KMG Financial Ltd/Patrick A McIntosh.)

Fig. 6.2. Lower Manhattan, New York City, has had difficulty adjusting to structural changes in employment. Rents have not changed for more than a decade and loft conversions to residential use are taking place.

Fig. 6.3. The Gateway of India, Bombay, a booming city and the financial capital of a country competing for jobs, particularly in the computer software sector, with Great Britain and other countries.

Fig. 6.4. New Delhi, India. The parliament buildings designed by Sir Edwin Lutyens in the closing days of the British Raj in the 1940s. The infrastructure of the city, created with public finance, provides the framework for the rapid growth of the private economy since India embarked upon financial deregulation.

values will go the same way as New York. For more than a decade now rental values in New York have hardly changed (Table 6.1). Although mid-town New York has recovered to some extent from the recession of the late 1980s, in parts of downtown Manhattan in the late 1990s more than 20% of office buildings remain vacant (Fig. 6.2).

A similar problem exists in Chicago, where rents are some of the lowest anywhere in the World yet downtown office vacancy still remains at around 20%. A number of office tenants have left the city in recent years, including Sears Roebuck who vacated the Sears Tower (the tallest in the world until

1996) in 1992 and moved 5000 staff out to Naperville, on the western side of the city. Suburban office vacancy levels have fallen much faster than in the downtown markets. As with Great Britain, out-of-town office locations are generally more in favour with office occupiers in the late 1990s. In 1996 suburban office markets witnessed their biggest fall in vacancy rates for 10 years. Back in 1970, 80% of office space in the USA's 50 largest metropolitan areas was located downtown; by 1994 this figure had fallen to 39%.

In the new world order we have a contrast between expanding cities of Asia, in the so-called Third World, compared with cities in mature economies of the First World, where a painful process of urban restructuring is underway.

Global financial deregulation

Ironically, the acceleration of economic growth in Asia has partly been caused by the deregulation of financial markets in the mature economies. During the 1970s, 'the big apple' got into severe financial difficulty and New York deregulated its financial markets. Financial deregulation was picked up by London in the mid-1980s and has now been copied by many economies throughout the world. For instance, financial deregulation – the process of removing restrictions on the movement of capital and the opening of markets to international finance – has contributed towards an explosion of economic activity in India. Bombay, the original home of the Dutch East Indies Company set up in 1610, has reasserted itself as one of the major financial cities of Asia (Fig. 6.3). However, the problems of physical congestion are enormous.

As with America or China, different cities will take on different roles and it is possible that Bombay will expand as the financial capital of India, leaving New Delhi (Fig. 6.4) to be the political, ceremonial and cultural hub of the country. The parliamentary buildings, and the layout of New Delhi designed by Edwin Lutyens in the 1940s, are a legacy of an earlier period of world economic activity when 'Pax Britannica' and the Gold Standard ruled the waves and created economic stability. But it is the area of information technology, with a software industry turnover of $1.2 billion, that India is changing dramatically. Software exports have emerged as the highest net foreign exchange earner, with companies like Novell, Microsoft, Oracle, Motorola, Texas Instruments and Siemens establishing in cities like Bangalore. Companies like BT, BA and Avis buy software from India, at the expense of jobs in Britain and other parts of Europe.

Privatisation and the striving for efficiency

In the early 1980s, in an endeavour to 'roll back the powers of the state', a programme of privatization commenced in Great Britain. What started as a political creed in Great Britain has become a world-wide necessity in developed and developing economies. In a world of increasing global competition, both the public and private sectors of the economies have to behave efficiently. The privatization of a number of corporations such as British Telecommunications, British Airways and the Rover Car Company has resulted in dramatic improvements in efficiency. This privatization trend has taken place in parallel with a programme of corporate 're-engineering', with companies such as BT down-sizing the number employed from over 245 000 in 1990 to less than 137 000 in 1995.

In the private sector, large international corporations have also been 're-engineered'. ABB the Swiss–Swedish engineering company, guided by Percy Barnevik, has downsized the number of headquarters staff from 2000 to 200. IBM have downsized their staff from over 300 000 world wide in 1992 to 200 000 in 1995. In early 1996 AT&T announced they were to lose 40 000 staff from a total workforce of 300 000 world wide. The striving for efficiency in both the private and public sectors, in an increasingly competitive global market, continues and will have an important impact on the future of world cities. Town and cities will have to become more efficient to compete internationally, particularly as multinational companies decentralize power and empower local companies. For ABB the strategy is for a federation of companies to be answerable both to the company and to the region of the world in which they operate. The matrix of responsibilities puts pressure on towns and cities to compete for their employment.

This striving for efficiency, and the downsizing of the public sector, has now become a world-wide political creed. It is suggested by Michael Prowse of the *Financial Times* that by 'a commitment to capitalism, the US ensured the survival of a broadly free market global system during decades when nearly all of Europe's intellectuals were bitterly opposed . . .'.

In his recent book *The World After Communism* Lord Skidelsky, as mentioned in Chapter 2, has suggested that there had been a struggle between the forces of 'liberalism' against 'collectivism' in the twentieth century. Collectivism (in the form of communism) had now failed. Skidelsky suggests: 'The financial rule (discipline) needs to be supported by what I would call an "anti-collectivist" rule . . . that public spending should not exceed 30% of national income.' The thesis is that somehow nations are more efficient if they rely on private rather than public expenditure. It is suggested one has only to look at Asia, where public expenditure is much lower than in Europe and private savings often much higher, to see the effect on economic growth. We are then left with this dilemma: How should the 30% be spent? How do we distinguish between public expenditure on social necessities such as healthcare, and social expenditure on education and transport infrastructure, which may be required as both a social necessity and an investment for future national financial returns? Skidelsky does not distinguish between the need for public expenditure in mature versus immature economies; nor does he question whether economic inefficiency creates a need for public expenditure. Reducing public expenditure may not, by itself, automatically create greater efficiency, particularly in town and city centres.

Lord Skidelsky also does not address the issue that the cheapest form of finance is from the public sector; if one relies on private finance, due to the associated risks of private investment, the cost of that finance will be more expensive. In other words, the productivity gains from 'privatization' may in some instances be more than offset by the inefficiencies of the higher cost of private capital.

This discussion goes to the heart of the UK Private Finance Intiative; it may be possible to use private finance in the public sector, but the productivity gains will only be achieved if the public sector, in procuring privately financed facilities, is clear in its requirements. If the public sector in any country does not clarify its requirement as the occupier of an office building, hospital, library or similar facility, the private investment risks will rise and the cost of finance increase, eroding the national productivity gains from involving the private sector.

Linked to this issue of using the private market and public sector projects, *The Economist* magazine wrote in 1994: 'It is no coincidence that the biggest increases in income inequality have occurred where free market economic policies have been pursued most zealously'. As discussed in Chapter 2, between 1969 and 1992 the household incomes of the top 20% of Americans have increased from 7.5 to 11 times the poorest 20%. In Britain, between 1977 and 1991, the top 20% of household incomes have jumped from a multiplier of 4 to 7 times the poorest 20%. As the United Nations Development Programme has identified, there have also been winners and losers in the world economy; some countries have become proportionally richer than others.

Not surprisingly there are those who do not follow the Skidelsky thesis. It was Professor J.K. Galbraith who suggested in his book in the 1950s that an 'affluent society' might create 'an atmosphere of private opulence and public squalor' with the growth of private car ownership, poor urban roads and an inadequate public transport system. This is a theme Galbraith has revisited in *The Good Society* in 1996. Galbraith also suggested that the private sector does not necessarily seek to maximize profit but aims to minimize risk; in other words, competitive economies increasingly move towards the domination of the marketplace by a few players who seek long-term income security rather than short-term profits.

This dilemma is writ large in Great Britain following, for instance, the privatization of the bus companies. Increasing merger and acquisition since privatisation has resulted in the number of private bus company operators diminishing to a situation where a public monopoly has been replaced by an oligopoly of private bus company operators. This is a world trend with the agglomeration of activity into fewer world players, including companies involved in TV, media, utilities, car construction and merchant banking.

Professor Galbraith suggests that to reduce public spending, as suggested by Skidelsky, to create national economic efficiency may not be a sound argument. He states that: 'The rich . . . do not want to defend themselves as rich. They want to have a larger moral case . . . something that seems on the whole vaguely plausible.'

This discussion between the merits of public and private expenditure goes to the heart of the future towns and cities across the world. Paris in France, Brazilia in Brazil, Canberra in Australia and, of course, Washington DC in America – as well as places like Milton Keynes, Cumbernauld and Canary Wharf in Great Britain – represent cities and urban areas that have been created with the aid of public finance. Could any of these cities, and many more towns and urban areas, have been created if the world had followed Lord Skidelsky's creed and reduce public expenditure to a minimal level? Is the growing level of urban congestion of cities in Asia a result of an inadequate public expenditure on transport infrastructure? Thailand may soon impose severe restrictions on the use of new private cars in traffic-congested Bangkok, yet Jakara and Bombay also suffer from severe traffic problems.

The Interstate Highway Act of 1956 in America is an event which might not have taken place without public expenditure. This was an Act brought about by President Dwight Eisenhower and created a network of federally subsidized highways, connecting major urban centres, that was justified, like most other projects in the 1950s, as a national defence measure. Between 1945 and 1980, 75% of all Federal Funds for transportation were spent on highways, rather than public transport (which is why, by the 1990s, America had one of the best long-distance road systems in the world and perhaps the poorest infrastructure of public transport).

Here we have, in President Eisenhower, one of the major contradictions in twentieth-century politics; a Republican president, in theory preaching the same sermon on public expenditure as Lord Skidelsky, and believing in the concept of a balanced budget, spending vast sums of public money on a transport network. In the 1930s John Maynard Keynes had suggested that public expenditure could stimulate the private sector economies. He put forward his theory of the expenditure multiplier by saying: 'Estimate what proportion of typical expenditure becomes some (else's) income, and what proportion of this income is then spent.' But by the 1970s it was thought that Keynesian economics was partly to blame for the high levels of inflation. The irony was that in the 1980s another Republican president, President Ronald Reagan, commenced the same exercise. Known as the 'great communicator' he created both a huge public sector debt and an enormous balance of payment deficit which, as we know, contributed towards the global stock market crash of 1987. For yet another Republican President to behave in this way was extraordinary. As John Kenneth Galbraith said in his book *The World Economy Since the War*, published in 1994: 'President Reagan was the most clearly committed Keynesian since the Kennedy years, perhaps since John Maynard Keynes himself.'

Reagan's expenditure created one of the largest American property booms of the twentieth century. In America it is estimated about 70% of all office space today was created in this period. In the United Kingdom a property boom was created by slightly different events. In the early 1980s Milton Friedman, the arch-duke of monetary theory, visited Downing Street to explain how monetary theory worked. Monetary theory has echoes of Albert Einstein's theory of relativity which states:

$$E = mc^2$$
Energy = Mass $\times$ Speed of light, squared

At the heart of monetary theory is another simple equation. The 'quantity theory of money' simply states:

$$MV = PY$$

The money stock in the economy (*M*), multiplied by the velocity of circulation, (*V*) is equal to the level of prices in an economy (*P*) multiplied by the volume of income of output (*Y*).

Having taken this apparently elegant and simple idea from Friedman, it was with some surprise that the UK government allowed the economy, and the property market, to grow out of control through the 1980s. In the early 1980s the annual growth of money (M4) was increasing at around 10%, yet by 1989 M4 was growing by nearly 20% per year. It is not surprising, with the stock of money increasing so dramatically, that there was a property boom; the banks had plenty of money to lend. During this period more than a third of all office buildings in the City of London were replaced.

Nigel Lawson, the Chancellor of the Exchequer in Margaret Thatcher's government for much of the 1980s, says in *The View from No. 11*: 'My central mistake was undoubtedly to underestimate the strength and duration of the boom of the late 1980s.' Lawson suggested that there were four things which had not been fully understood:

1. The imprudent nature of lending institutions following financial deregulations.
2. The sharp fall in sterling exchange rate in 1986.
3. The overreaction to the 1987 stock market crash.
4. The belated depreciation of overheating in 1988.

The Reagan/Thatcher 1980s economic boom also created the most enormous property boom that the world has ever known, which had an impact across the developed world with cities like Frankfurt and Paris, as well as cities in southern Europe such as Madrid, and cities such as Sydney and Perth (Fig. 6.5) experiencing enormous rental and capital growth. In Paris the Grande Arch at La Defense appeared, Frankfurt saw the speculative Messeturm built and the

Fig. 6.5. Perth, Western Australia, suffered dramatically as a result of the property boom of the 1980s. Along with many other Anglo-Saxon world cities, it started the 1990s with an excessive supply of new buildings but no demand. Demand has partially recovered in recent years.

dramatic twin leaning towers of the Pueta de Europa were incomplete at the end of the boom in Madrid in 1990 as the developer was bankrupt.

The new world order . . .

In the late 1990s we are now in a period where, to some extent, there has been a cyclical recovery from the boom of the 1980s and the recession of the early 1990s. However, the world has changed; international competition is constraining governments and central banks such as the Federal Reserve Board in the USA, the Bundesbank in Germany or the Bank of England. The demands for financial rectitude of the European Maastricht Treaty are part of this new order. There are also major structural changes taking place, largely brought on by financial deregulation (pioneered by the USA and UK). The success of the Uruguay Round of negotiations to achieve the General Agreement of Tariffs and Trade resulting in the World Trade Organization, the strive for productivity gains and the growing use of information technology have accelerated this trend. In many cities, the result has been that rents have hardly altered during the 1990s, and in some cities, such as New York, rents are lower in nominal terms than they were in 1986. In real terms they are even lower, as shown in Table 6.1.

The lack of rental growth in many mature cities around the world is a reflection of the lack of inflation. Over the last 30 years real estate development has been significantly influenced by rental and capital inflationary changes. As Roger Bootle explains in *The Death of Inflation*, those days are gone: 'The western world is in the grip of overwhelming forces which are transforming the economic and business landscape and the lives of ordinary people.' Bootle suggests that for two generations inflation has been the 'Great Deceiver'. This is particularly true of property development in towns and cities across the world. Investors, developers, town planners and many more have been able to hide their mistakes behind inflationary gains. No more. The low inflationary world is unforgiving and far more competitive, requiring a far deeper understanding of how towns and cities will compete and survive in the future.

Table 6.1 World office rents

	1976	1986	1992	1996	Change % 1992–96
London: City (ft^2 p.a.)	14.25	37.50	37.50	37.50	0
West End (ft^2 p.a.)	9.50	28.00	42.50	42.50	0
New York (US$): midtown (ft^2 p.a.)	14.00	52.50	47.00	47.75	0
downtown (ft^2 p.a.)	14.00	39.00	31.00	31.00	0
Chicago (US$) (ft^2 p.a.)	13.70	26.50	30.00	30.50	0
Paris (FF) (m^2 p.a.)	900.00	2800.00	4300.00	3000.00	−30
Frankfurt (DM) (m^2 p.m.)	22.00	36.00	77.50	55.00	−30
Sydney (A$) (m^2 p.a.)	102.00	450.00	650.00	610.00	−7
Singapore (A$) (m^2 p.m.)	2.00	3.20	7.41	9.93	+34
Hong Kong (HK$) (m^2 p.m.)	9.50	26.00	43.00	67.43	+56
Tokyo (Yen) (m^2 p.m.)	9300.00	13000.00	25800.00	15400.00	−42
Jakarta US$) (m^2 p.a.)	13.00	8.00	12.00	12.00	0
Madrid (Pts) (m^2 p.m.)	825.00	2200.00	5500.00	2600.00	−50

Source: Richard Ellis World Rents Survey – various dates.

Towns and cities across the world are changing as they compete for global business. Professor Jeremy Rifkin, President of the Foundation of Economic Trends in Washington DC in his book *The End of Work*, suggests: 'Political parties throughout the world are not addressing what is going to be their No.1 issue. We are moving into the information age; computers and robots are replacing whole job categories.' Rifkin also suggests that by the year 2025 only 2% of the world's workforce (not just in America!) will be blue collar factory workers; the global job market is changing at an alarming rate.

In parallel with this dramatic change in work patterns, we have an explosion in the number of old people. The 'demographic timebomb' is exploding bit by bit, year by year. As discussed in Chapter 2, in the UK less than 5% of the population is over 80, but by 2050 around 10% of the population will be over 80! In the mature economies generally, around 30% of the population will be over 60 by the middle of the next century. We are therefore left with the scenario that information technology is taking over jobs in cities across the world, yet there are more and more mouths to feed, with fewer and fewer people in full-time employment.

Cities of the world will change dramatically. Professor Rifkin suggests that we need to stop thinking in terms of the 'public sector' or the 'private sector' but consider a third sector. This he calls the 'civic sector' where more and more employment will be neither public nor private but will be labour intensive. For instance, running nursery schools or sports clubs or old people's homes requires labour. In Great Britain over the last 15 years the numbers employed in education, health, social work and other community activities has increased by 28%. Similar trends are occurring in the USA. These are typical of the employment growth sectors of the mature economies in the twenty-first century and our property markets across the globe will change dramatically to reflect this trend.

... and the location of employment

The polarization of wealth referred to earlier, and its implications for employment, are now reflected in the property market. The core of many cites epitomized in London by the NatWest Tower in the City of London or Canary Wharf, will remain important locations for employment, and hence property investment values will be maintained. For instance, the Lloyds Underwriters building will prove to be a very sound investment for the German Pension Fund who recently acquired it. However, increasingly jobs will follow people, not the other way round. The issue for the mature economies across the world in the late twentieth century is: Where do people want to live and work, particularly the meritocratic élite whose employment is linked to the concept of 'intellectual property'?

Over a number of years The Harris Research Centre and Healey & Baker have conducted a survey of European businesses. As one of the original creators of this survey, one critical question I and others wanted to ask was: 'What city do you think is best in terms of quality of life for employees?' Paris, Munich, Barcelona, Geneva and Zurich perform well, but the results show that although London is in the top ten, it is consistently outside the top five. Other cities such as Frankfurt, Berlin, Hamburg, Lyon, Milan and Amsterdam are also missing from the top of this league table. Where people want to live is increasingly where they want to work.

Around London there is a clear distinction between west London and east London. As discussed in Chapter 5, since 1990 virtually all the office market activity has been on the west side of London in the Thames Valley, such as Stockley Park, reflecting the location where staff want to live and hence where people want to work.

This is the phenomenon noted in America with companies leaving town centres and moving jobs to the suburbs where people want to live and work. For instance, office space is in very short supply in Burbank, on the edge of Los Angeles, yet 20% of the old downtown market remains empty. I referred to Chicago and New York earlier, where a similar trend is apparent.

In an article entitled 'Great Escape from the City' in the *Financial Times* in October 1996, the choice of which surburb to relocate to was summed up as: 'wherever the president of the company lives'. Most presidents don't wish to live downtown. However, Seattle and San Francisco, on the west coast are winning: Seattle is the home of Boeing and Microsoft while San Francisco is adjacent to Palo Alto and Silicon Valley (Fig. 6.6). Both cities demonstrate preferred locations for the international meritocratic élite in the age of information technology. But in America there is also the concept of 'comeback cities' such as Baltimore, Cincinnati, Cleveland, Columbus, Denver, New Orleans, San Diego and Tampa where new life has been breathed into the urban areas by adding culture facilities, entertainment districts, government facilities, hospitals and universities.

Philadelphia is an example of what can be achieved. Mayor Edward G. Rendell, who called for a 'new urban agenda', has pioneered a programme of 'urban re-engineering' involving a long-range plan to revitalize neighbourhoods to bring culture and investment back into the city centre. Other cities such as

Fig. 6.6. The Skyline of San Francisco, California. The city appeals to the meritocratic élite of the late twentieth century. It is located close to Palo Alto, a major centre for software creation employment, and within the fastest growing state in the USA.

125

Dallas, Chicago, Houston, downtown New York and Los Angeles are likely to see downtown rents fall in real terms as they lose out to new suburban locations. Tax incentives, however, are encouraging some buildings to be converted to residential use in a few cities.

To some extent the polarization of employment activity has happened in Paris; La Defence has become a popular location, but so are the western suburbs of Versailles, St Germain en Laye and St Quentin. Marne la Vallée in the east, as with the east side of London or Berlin, is not favoured by the meritocratic élite of the late twentieth century.

The 'underclass' cultures which have grown up in parts of London, Paris and all large cities, including the south side of Chicago or around Washington, DC, where the meritocratic élite prefer not to live, pose the greatest challenge for cities in the next century. These problems of poverty are even greater in cities such as Moscow and Johannesburg, both of which are beginning to develop international reputations for their levels of crime. Within cities, and between cities across the world, there is a polarization of wealth. The costs of crime and corruption in all town and cities may increase costs and make such locations less efficient – an important issue in a competitive world economy.

The dilemma for the future of cities may best be illustrated by Berlin and Prague. In Berlin there is the major challenge to integrate the two halves of the

Fig. 6.7. Brandenburg Park, south of Berlin, Germany. A development which has avoided the legal and political constraints of central Berlin, providing 220 hectares of landscaped industrial and business space suitable for the next millennium. (Photograph: Horsham Properties GmbH/Trizec Hahn of Canada.)

city; the eastern half (like London and Paris) has always been regarded as the poorer side of the city but has been 'privatized' since the Berlin wall was demolished in 1989. Like many cities, the centre is not regarded as an efficient place for employment in the late twentieth century. Rental values for office buildings fell by 50% in the five years to 1996. Although the shopping centre at Friedrichstrasse, including Galeries Lafayette, is complete, other much discussed schemes at Unter den Linden and Potsdammer Platz in the centre of the city are far from complete. However, the construction of the Brandenburg Park (Fig. 6.7), a major new location for businesses on the south side of the city, by Horsham Properties, now part of Trizec Hahn of Canada, has very successfully managed to avoid the congestion, legal and political problems associated with new development within the old city centre.

As anyone who has conducted business in any of the cities within the former Soviet Empire knows, the lack of a clear legal infrastructure (and corruption at all levels of the law) can be a major problem for investment. The inability of

Fig. 6.8. The Charles Bridge, Prague in the Czech Republic, a city which attracts residents and visitors, and is able to compete successfully for meritocratic employment in the late 1990s. (Photograph: T. Sibova.)

some former Soviet Empire citizens to understand how the private investment market assesses investment risk, would appear to be only an extreme version of the inabilities of a number of town planners in Great Britain!

The success of the Czech Republic in privatizing itself and adjusting from a 'command economy' under communism to a 'market economy' in the new world order where labour productivity increased by over 18% in 1995, is epitomized by Prague (Fig. 6.8). Prague, like other cities across the world, such as San Francisco, offers a unique visual and cultural setting attracting both residents and tourists, and hence employment. Here is surely the secret for success for cities in the next century; if people want to live in and visit a city, employment will follow, particularly the international meritocratic élite. The true success will come when people want to move back into the centre of towns and cities – a phenomenon which is beginning to take place in New York and in central London. For instance, parts of the old County Hall building, the former home of the Greater London Council, as discussed in Chapter 2, have been transformed into residential apartments.

Entertainment may hold the key; as discussed in Chapter 4, in Cleveland, Columbus and Cincinnati the strategy has been to turn the city inside out. As people, retailing and employment have left the centres, the centres have become the locations for major entertainment projects such as ball parks, a Rock and Roll Hall of Fame, hotels, stadiums and convention centres. Locating the Olympic Games in Atlanta in 1996 also demonstrated part of a winning strategy. It is claimed that 1595 US and 364 international companies have moved to Atlanta over the last 10 years. By winning the Olympic Games for the year 2000, Sydney in Australia (Fig. 6.9) is also hoping it will help the city establish a new position in a competitive world.

The future
Throughout the world different towns and cities, competing with each other in the new world order, have different agendas to follow.

- The challenge for cities in the First World – of Western Europe and North America – will be to adjust to an epoch of fewer full-time jobs in the office sector, a polarization of wealth and an ageing population. If they do not face up to these structural changes, their spiritual and financial wealth will decline.
- The challenge for cities in the Second World – such as those formerly within the Soviet Empire – will not only be to recognize the problems associated with cities in the First World, but also to recognize that a clear legal and political infrastructure is essential for their orderly urban development.
- The challenge for cities in the Third World will be to recognize the mistakes (and successes) of cities in the First World. In 1996 the Petronas Towers in Kuala Lumpa (Fig. 6.10) became the tallest buildings in the world, even taller than the Sears Tower in Chicago. In 1997 work starts on Gigawold, the world's largest building along 1.8 km of the River Klang in Kuala Lumpur.

Fig. 6.9. Sydney Harbour, Australia. A focal point for a country competing for employment, aided by being chosen as the city for the Olympic Games in 2000.

Are the booming cities of Asia, including Shanghai, Jakarta, Seoul and Bangkok, repeating the mistakes and problems which now exist in mature cities like Chicago, New York, Paris and London? Speculation in cities like Manila in the Philipines has been at an extraordinary level and property prices have trebled in only three years. São Paulo demonstrates a different problem; the 5 million road vehicles are responsible for 90% of the 3 million tons of polluting gases and particles deposited into the city every year!

Jean Claude Paye, in *The OECD Observer* summed up the issue:

> Urban living conditions define the quality of life for more than half of mankind and increasingly affect the lifestyles and opportunities available to people in rural regions as well.

In the same report, Josef W. Konvitz stated:

> The ease of relocating economic activities from one place to another means that cities have to offer business something more than access to a supply of labour, resources and market. Cities want to draw attention to the high quality of life they can offer, through investment, innovation and the institutions they contain.

The process of redefining the role of cities was neatly summed up by Lewis Mumford in his book *The City in History*, published in 1961. He said:

129

Fig. 6.10. The Petronas Towers, Kuala Lumpur, Malaysia, which became the tallest office buildings in the world in 1996. But are the fast-growing cities of Asia becoming too congested and repeating the mistakes of the mature economies? (Photograph: Don Head, De Montfort University, Milton Keynes.)

The key function of the city is to convert power into form, energy into culture, dead matter into living symbols of art, biological reproduction into social creativity. The positive functions of the city cannot be performed without creating new institutional arrangements, capable of coping with the vast energies modern man now commands. . . .

In an increasingly competitive world, it is clear that the management of cities will become more important. The powerful forces of the global economy will punish the disorganized. Public and private sectors must work in harmony if cities are to survive and prosper in the next millennium.

CHAPTER 7

Property investment and its influence on urban change

In the last years of the nervous 1990s, it is difficult to remember that 1982 was a turning point in the history of the commercial property investment market in the last half century. This was the year when, after more than a decade, the yield on long-dated government bonds became positive; from 1982 the financial world re-entered a period of real interest rates (Fig. 7.1). Despite this change, for a variety of reasons, it took the property investment market almost 10 years to appreciate the significance of this event. Many urban town planners remain unaware or have not appreciated the importance of this change, but town and city development will depend upon a working relationship, as well as an understanding, between the public and private sectors.

Facts and figures to understand urban change
Before examining the impact that public and private sources of money have on the commercial property investment market and urban change, it is worth

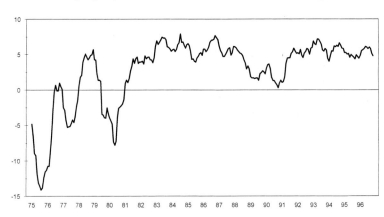

Fig. 7.1. Real gilt yields since 1975. Since 1982 nominal gilt yields (for long-dated stocks) have exceeded inflation in every year. The years of negative real yields are past. (Source: Office for National Statistics/ Financial Times.)

reviewing the facts and figures now available to all those involved with urban property investment and town planning. This should be an aid to better decision making.

Demographic data

Over the last decade there has been a quiet revolution in the way that data is handled. The impact of information technology has reached the urban scenes. The most profound change is the understanding we now have of demography; a large number of organizations now provide databases demonstrating demographic change and demographic profiles at a regional, town and even post-code level. Examples of two urban locations were discussed in Chapter 2. Such companies as CACI with their Acorn profile, the Unit for Retailing Planning Information in Reading (widely used in Planning Appeals), CES Limited and CCN with their Mosaic analysis, all provide a far deeper understanding of the residential and working catchment population of any location within Great Britain. CCN also provide an international database, although a number of governments are far worse at providing accurate demographic information than Great Britain; the 10-yearly population census is not too accurate in many other countries. In this country town planning and urban property investors have a distinct advantage; they are now able to quantify population change in both size and profile.

Economic trends

A second area where data is available relates to regional and town level forecasts. Oxford Economic Forecasting with their regional team Northern Ireland Economic Research, Cambridge Econometrics and Business Strategies Limited all provide analyses and outlooks for different industrial sectors and geographic areas which should be part of any assessment of the relative performance of competing towns and cities.

Property market statistics

The third dramatic change in databases has occurred in the property investment market. Following a series of events, such as the property crash of the early 1970s, a large number of firms of property consultants now provide a wide range of data to understand how the market is changing. Jones Lang Wootton was one of the earliest firms to produce a property investment performance index. Hillier Parker May & Rowden also pioneered a programme of tracking rental change for prime (the best) rental values in the market. Both these databases came into existence in the mid-1970s, and were closely followed by a regular report on prime property investment yields from Healey & Baker. A number of other organizations, such as DTZ Debenham Thorpe, King Sturge, Weatherall Green & Smith, Michael Laurie & Partners, Knight Frank, St Quintin, Chesterton and Grimley JR Eve, have also produced regular market information over the years.

The urban planning system in Great Britain surely has the best set of socio-economic and property market data of any country in the world, yet there still seems to be a misunderstanding as to how and why urban change takes place.

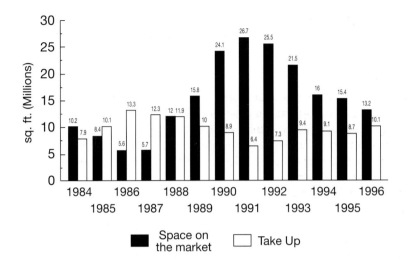

Fig. 7.2. Central London office availability and take-up for 1984–96 shows the fall in the number of empty office buildings from over 26 million ft² in 1991. Take-up has also recovered from the low point of only 6.4 million ft² in the same year. (Source: Richard Ellis.)

Richard Ellis is unique among property consultants in two respects: not only was it one of the earliest organizations to pioneer the concept of property investment performance measurement, but it also still provides the earliest indicator of direct property investment performance of any country in the world. The Richard Ellis Monthly Index appears within the first seven days of any month, reflecting the changes in rental, capital and total performance over the previous month. Having produced this index over a number of years, it is with some surprise how little notice is taken of such material.

In addition to major firms of surveyors producing data on the property market, London Residential Research (as discussed in Chapter 2) has recently starting tracking all major residential schemes in central London, particularly where office buildings are being converted into residential use. This complements the office databases produced by a number of surveyors. For instance, Richard Ellis tracks every office building in central London having more than 1000 ft² (Fig. 7.2), and also tracks all office buildings in towns around the M25 motorway, as well as in major regional capitals such as Birmingham, Leeds, Manchester, Liverpool and Glasgow.

Stock market analysis

The UK property market is also unique in having a large number of stock brokers who provide commentary, not only on the above sets of data, but also on share price movements; in other words, they monitor indirect property investment performance. Such firms as SG Warburg, UBS, BZW, Merryll Lynch (formerly Smith NewCourt), HSBC, James Capel, NatWest, Kleinwort Benson and others contribute to what must be the nearest thing to perfect information on the property investment market of any country in the world.

On-line systems

Two other major events have taken place over the last 15 years which also make the British property market stand out as unique. Property Intelligence Plc provide their FOCUS system which is an on-line database tracking all known (published) property announcements as well as rateable values for 1990 and 1995, auction results, local and structure plans and demographic data. Their City Wise service also provides a list of occupiers suitable for a wide range of applications. This complements other on-line systems such as Pro-Vision and PRIDE, which track respectively London office availability, and industrial and office availability outside London. The *Estates Gazette Interactive* (EGi) using the Internet has also recently become available, as has *Property Link* which markets commercial buildings on the Internet.

Investment data

In terms of direct property investment performance, complementing the information provided by on-line systems and surveyors, the Investment Property Databank (IPD) provides not only a unique but the most comprehensive set of information on the property investment market which is the envy of investors and developers in countries beyond the shores of Great Britain. IPD, in their *Property Investors Digest* for 1996, states that records include:

- A building description and ownership record, including location, building type, age, date of purchase and method of acquisition.
- An annual financial record, taking in valuation information at the year-end, plus all capital and income flows through the year.
- A full tenancy record, detailing the type of occupier, lease terms, floor space, rental flows and lease terms.
- All investment portfolios included in the Databank are tracked back in full to December 1980 wherever possible. All properties bought and sold through those fifteen years are recorded, to give a complete picture of returns and investment activity through the whole period.

    At December 1995, the Databank held records on 12 300 properties, with a floor area of 460 million square feet, accommodating some 63 000 tenants. The total value of £47.9 billion in equivalent to three-quarters of the property owned by UK insurance and pension funds (as measured by the Government statistics). Records are also held on 15 000 properties held at some point in the last 15 years but sold before the end of 1995.

The size of the market

We have in Great Britain an extraordinary situation: we have more information on the property investment market than exists elsewhere, yet we have a town planning system which frequently misunderstands urban change. However, the information which is available generally relates to a relatively small part of the property market – the institutional investment property market – but it does at least provide clear signs to trends in the property market generally.

    IPD has calculated that the total value of UK commercial property is £265 bn, representing 9% of the total wealth of the economy, compared to residential buildings which account 41% of all wealth. However, the total asset value of all buildings monitored by IPD (£47.9 million in 1995) is still a relatively small percentage of the national balance sheet, as set out in Table 7.1. The table demonstrates that property forms the majority of all assets held by individuals and companies in Great Britain. However, one has to add an element of caution;

Tangible assets	1985	1990	1995
Residential buildings	626.6	270.6	217.7
Agricultural land, buildings and forestry	36.4	40.2	40.8
Commercial buildings	163.9	305.1	265.2
Industrial buildings	25.9	37.6	32.1
Other buildings	100.9	141.6	134.5
Civil engineerings works	157.6	229.7	254.2
Plant and machinery	239.1	335.0	441.1
Ships, aircraft and railway rolling stock	8.9	6.3	7.2
Road vehicles	18.1	27.4	30.4
Stocks and work in progress	88.8	118.1	134.1
Total tangible assets	1466.2	2511.6	2557.3

Source: Office for National Statistics.

Table 7.1 National balance sheets

the United Kingdom national accounts calculates these figures primarily from the Inland Revenue Rating Lists of market rental values. Current figures relate to 1988 but data is revalued every five years, the most recent list being dated April 1993.

To arrive at a capital figure, these rental values are converted using a capitalization ratio, based upon a sample survey of 1000 buildings conducted by the Valuation Offices in 1992. Earlier capitalization ratios were based upon interpolated data from 1976 and 1985. Herein lies one of the anomalies of urban land management; while private individuals and commercial organizations are aware of their asset worth (for instance such figures appear on balance sheets), the public sector is unaware of its market value, or how those capital values are changing over time as a result of policy decisions and their implementation, or general market movements.

Influences shaping the property investment market

The above data clearly demonstrates that properties owned as investment assets form an important element of the British economy. Pension Funds and Life Assurance companies are important investors yet the growth of the institutional property market, certainly in its extent, is unique to Great Britain. This is an issue described by John Plender in his book *That's the Way the Money Goes* in 1982, in which he likened the institutions to the Leviathans of the financial world.

Behind its growth is the striving for economic efficiency; all markets reflect, over the longer term, this correcting mechanism. While the demand for buildings, the growth of affluence, the greater mobility of a car-owning democracy and the impact of technology (such as telephones and computers) has an impact, major financial pressures actually shape investment markets. The property investment market is no exception.

In *A Guide to Institutional Property Investment* in the 1980s I discussed the suggestion that the UK institutional property investment market had been shaped by inflation. However, this simplistic analysis does not explain why a number of commercial owner occupiers over the last half century in the UK have become leasehold occupiers. Owner occupation rather than leasehold occupation is far higher in most other European countries.

There are a number of advantages to being an owner occupier, such as being able to influence the design of the building you occupy and enjoying the asset value growth (which can contribute to a company's positive balance sheet). Owners also benefit from taxation allowances on capital assets owned, as well as being able to offset annual bank loan/mortgage costs against tax. However, since the Second World War a number of occupiers in the UK have realized that owning buildings results in tying up capital in assets which could be invested in other areas of business. There is a realization that buildings fall in value in terms of asset depreciation and building obsolescence and that purchasing and selling capital assets can be a heavy financial burden, as can the management of a building owned for occupation. Over the decades an enormous property investment industry in the UK has evolved, including investors, developers and bankers, as well as professions involved with the industry such as chartered surveyors, lawyers, architects and property consultants generally. In other words, the property investment industry has evolved separately from the property construction industry, although there are close links between the two.

The influence of monetary policy

One of the principal contributors to the growth of the property investment industry has been monetary policy, or the lack of it, over the last half century. The UK economy has been categorized, as shown in Table 7.2, by a series of booms and credit squeezes. One of the earliest occurred after the relaxation of building licences in 1951. The immediate post-war government had introduced not only taxation on development rights, but also required Building Licences before construction could start. This was at a time when the economy was growing from the period of wartime austerities. When the government changed in the early 1950s, Building Licences were revoked and the property investment market took off, but between 1950 and 1952 the bank rate doubled from 2% to 4%. A similar event took place in 1954 when the interest rate was 3%, but was later increased and reached 7% by 1957.

The volatility of interest rates has been one of the principal characteristics of the UK economy, particularly compared with the German economy, in the post-war period. The property investment market has grown partly in response to this situation, an issue I discussed at the RICS 'Cutting Edge' conference in 1994. For instance, in 1972 bank base rate was only 4.5%, yet by 1977 it had reached 17%. This followed the enormous property boom of 1972–74 and the property crash in 1974 following the oil crisis at the end of 1973. History repeated itself in the late 1980s when interest rates briefly fell as low as 7% in 1987 but then increased dramatically to 15% by 1990.

The behaviour of the financial markets in response to monetary policy influenced and encouraged property investment by institutions. At times when it was difficult to obtain bank finance, particularly in the 1960s and 1970s, life insurance companies and pension funds frequently came to the rescue; they provided finance for developers, as well as occupiers, to create buildings for occupation. The financial institutions, however, quickly realized that mortgage finance was unsatisfactory; the financial gains of the 1960s were being enjoyed by the developers and/or occupiers rather than the lenders of finance. Institutions therefore become equity participants and in many cases finished up

	UK ordinary shares	Bank base rate/MLR	Gilt yield*	Retail prices inflation	Prime shops	Prime offices	Prime industrial
1950	5.50	2.00	4.50	3.00	5.50	6.50	
1951	6.00	2.50	4.00	9.10	5.25	6.50	
1952	5.50	4.00	4.25	9.30	5.50	6.50	
1953	7.25	3.25	4.00	3.10	5.50	6.50	
1954	7.00	3.00	3.75	1.80	5.50	7.00	
1955	6.25	4.50	4.50	5.10	5.50	7.00	
1956	6.25	5.50	4.75	5.00	5.50	8.00	
1957	7.00	7.00	5.00	3.90	5.50	7.50	
1958	7.00	5.50	5.00	3.00	5.50	7.50	
1959	7.00	6.00	5.00	0.60	6.00	7.50	10.00
1960	5.00	7.00	5.25	1.00	5.50	7.00	10.00
1961	4.75	7.00	6.25	3.40	5.50	7.00	10.00
1962	5.50	6.00	6.25	4.20	5.50	6.60	10.00
1963	5.75	4.00	6.00	2.00	5.50	6.00	10.00
1964	5.00	7.00	5.50	3.30	5.50	7.00	10.00
1965	5.40	7.00	6.00	4.80	6.00	7.00	9.00
1966	5.50	7.00	6.50	3.90	6.00	6.50	9.00
1967	5.00	8.00	6.75	2.50	6.50	6.50	9.00
1968	3.60	8.00	8.00	4.70	7.00	7.00	9.00
1969	3.90	8.00	9.00	5.50	7.00	6.50	9.50
1970	4.40	8.00	9.00	6.40	7.50	7.50	9.00
1971	3.70	7.00	9.00	9.40	7.00	8.50	8.50
1972	3.11	9.00	9.36	7.10	6.00	5.50	7.50
1973	4.95	13.00	12.64	9.20	5.50	5.00	7.50
1974	12.04	11.50	16.32	16.00	8.00	8.00	10.00
1975	5.59	11.25	13.57	24.10	6.50	6.50	9.00
1976	6.89	14.25	16.17	16.80	6.00	6.50	9.00
1977	5.33	6.50	10.67	15.90	5.00	6.00	8.00
1978	5.65	12.50	13.11	8.20	4.00	4.50	6.25
1979	6.86	17.00	14.96	13.50	3.75	4.25	6.25
1980	6.09	14.00	13.78	18.00	3.75	4.50	6.25
1981	5.94	14.50	16.00	11.90	3.50	4.50	6.25
1982	5.30	10.00	11.58	8.60	3.90	4.90	6.75
1983	4.66	9.00	10.77	4.50	3.50	4.75	6.75
1984	4.51	9.50	10.98	5.00	3.50	4.75	6.75
1985	4.39	11.50	10.83	6.00	3.65	4.75	7.50
1986	4.10	11.00	10.79	3.40	4.00	4.75	8.25
1987	4.32	8.50	9.63	4.20	3.90	4.75	8.00
1988	4.71	13.00	9.76	4.90	4.50	4.75	7.50
1989	4.24	15.00	9.97	7.80	5.00	4.75	8.00
1990	5.47	14.00	10.68	9.40	5.25	5.00	9.50
1991	5.02	10.50	9.60	5.90	5.00	5.75	8.50
1992	4.35	7.00	8.56	3.80	5.50	6.50	8.50
1993	3.36	5.50	6.39	1.60	4.00	5.50	6.65
1994	4.02	6.25	8.71	2.50	4.25	4.75	6.50
1995	3.80	6.50	7.65	3.50	4.75	4.75	7.25
1996	3.80	6.00	7.82	2.10	5.00	4.50	7.00

* Consols 2.5% until 1972; 15-year medium coupon gilt thereafter.

Table 7.2 Investment yields and inflation, 1950–96

owning buildings. *Partners in Property* by B.P. Whitehouse and *The Property Boom* by Oliver Marriott provide englightening insights into the events of this period.

Asset strippers also began to dominate the market. Realizing there was an arbitrage gain to be made between the assets of companies valued using accountancy procedures (with historic values on their books) and the open market value of property, a number of companies and individuals gained financial rewards and dubious reputations in the 1970s from acquiring companies and selling on the assets at inflated prices by either closing the trading company or leasing back accommodation as occupiers.

The influence of property laws and finance acts

This programme, with the hidden hand of financial economic efficiency guiding the market, resulted in a number of other changes. The Law of Property Acts of 1922 and 1925 had provided an excellent framework for such investment activity. However, it was the Landlord and Tenants Acts of 1927 and 1954 which gave even greater legal certainty to the property investment markets. One of the anomalies which came out of the 1925 Act sets out the liabilities for taxation; lowest taxation is payable on leases granted for an unexpired term of more than 21 years. As inflation took off, the concept of rent reviews also evolved, but to avoid taxation leases had to be granted for more than 21 years. Five-year rent reviews became common, implying that lease lengths must be for 25 years to avoid taxation.

The Finance Acts of 1921 and 1965 also accelerated the involvement of rent-collecting property investors. The 1921 Act gave Pension Funds a tax advantage; they would be exempt from the taxation of investment income. The Finance Act of 1965 followed the Finance Act of 1961 and consolidated the issue of Capital Gains Tax. Capital Gains Tax penalized companies who paid out all their capital gains by dividends. Inevitably Life Insurance companies and Pension Funds became increasingly involved as this was the most efficient source of finance.

Increasingly, institutions dictated the speed of urban development and its design and the 'institutional lease' came into existence. Institutions wished to create a lease structure which minimized their investment risk and placed the full repair and maintenance (as well as insurance) liabilities on the tenant. Tenants were more than happy to comply with such impositions as this was logically the cheapest way of obtaining buildings for their own occupation.

These trends in the market caused by financial pressures and taxation enactments were reinforced by the planning system, at both a local and national level. The famous 'George Brown Ban' on office development (after the Labour Government Minister of that name) introduced the concept of Office Development Permits. These, together with Industrial Development Certificates, aimed to control urban development, against the wishes of the market. The result was that demand increased faster than supply, and investors enjoyed the enhanced capital and rental values which this market imbalance created, enabling institutions to become even more important as the owners of urban property.

Ironically, the reverse policy has appeared in the 1990s with John Gummer, as Secretary of State for the Environment, introducing a national restriction on out-of-town (rather than in-town) development, particularly retail development, in an attempt to 'protect' town centres. The effect on investment values is identical to the 1960s restrictions; out-of-town values continue to increase, making such investment by institutions and other even more attractive!

But what about town planners at a local level? Although they continued, throughout the 1960s and 1970s, to emphasize their role as 'town planners', in effect increasingly they were attempting to 'control' the market rather than 'plan' it; they had authority yet little power. The investing institutions had the money and the power; they cracked the whip in terms of leasehold occupation as well as town planning and urban development.

Property investment: the winners and losers

The evolution of the institutional property investment market, together with the databases which such a market has created, currently provides town planners with a vast amount of information – much of which could be used more effectively in town and city management. Town planners commonly regard 'the developer' as a necessary evil which has to be dealt with. Town planners have frequently been unable to appreciate that developers and investors are merely the intermediaries between, on the one hand, the needs of occupiers in a puralistic democratic market economy, and, on the other, town planners who seek to influence the shape of town and city development.

The concept of planning gains, previously under Section 52 of the 1971 Act and now under Section 106 of the 1990 Act, has become a quasi tax on urban developments, levied arbitrarily according to the negotiating strengths of the parties concerned. Such an ad-hoc system of urban taxation has only been possible due to enormous capital gains enjoyed from time to time over the period of the last three decades. It has resulted in some extraordinary urban development with social housing being built in the wrong place, and also arguably for the wrong purpose. Other examples have included community facilities (such as dance halls) being built adjacent to office buildings, or car park levies (referred to as commuted payments) being paid to planning authorities. This form of quasi taxation is in addition to other taxes on property, including income and corporation tax on rental income, capital gains tax, the uniform business rate, council tax, value added tax and stamp duty.

Occupier trends

The lack of understanding of the underlying demand for buildings from occupiers continues to this day. Present and future capital values are related to expectations of rental growth, and Table 7.3 sets out data provided by IPD of office rental value change in a sample of locations across Great Britain since 1980. The Table clearly indicates that almost all office locations have shown rental growth slower than inflation over 15 years and that office investment has therefore not generally been very successful. Perhaps even more surprising is that cities like Birmingham and Sheffield have shown far stronger rental growth than affluent locations such as Guildford and Basingstoke. Even the influence of Heathrow Airport has had an insignificant impact on the value of office

Hounslow	0.8%
Basingstoke	2.1%
Guildford	1.9%
Reading	1.0%
Birmingham	6.6%
Sheffield	5.2%
Inflation	6.1%

Table 7.3 Office rental value change: average p.a. 1980–95

Source: Investment Property Databank.

buildings in Hounslow. But why has Reading, in the affluent Thames Valley, seen such poor rental growth?

Table 7.4 shows that a similar pattern of rental change has emerged in the industrial market. Once again, we have the situation of no locations showing rental growth faster than inflation, yet locations such as Runnymede (on the M25 near Heathrow Airport) show far slower rental growth than Victorian industrial cities such as Birmingham and Sheffield.

Property investors and town planners have been slow to realize the impact of structural change in the UK economy and its negative impact on rental values. Table 7.5 indicates that the retail property market has also shown some extraordinary patterns of rental change. From the table it can be seen that affluent shopping locations such as Soho and Oxford Street South, or Knightsbridge (the home of Harrods!) have shown rental growth much slower than inflation, yet an industrial city such as Manchester has significantly outperformed inflation over a 15-year period.

Increasingly, more astute property investors are using such data at a town level, yet town planners often seem to be unaware of its existence or don't

Hounslow	3.3%
Basingstoke	4.3%
Reading	2.7%
Runnymeade	2.4%
Birmingham	4.5%
Sheffield	4.7%
Inflation	6.1%

Table 7.4 Industrial rental change: average p.a. 1980–95

Source: Investment Property Databank.

Chester	8.2%
Liverpool	4.1%
Manchester	7.3%
Macclesfield	6.6%
Knightsbridge	4.8%
Soho and Oxford Street South	4.0%
Inflation	6.1%

Table 7.5 Retail rental value change: average p.a. 1980–95

Source: Investment Property Databank.

	% Yes
Hotels	20
Public house	30
Out-of-town fastfood	51
Golf complexes	1
Factory outlets	47
Residential	20
University buildings	18
Hospital/health	13

Table 7.6 Is there a place in your portfolio for non-institutional properties?

Source: Baring, Houston & Saunders, Issue No. 144, November 1996.

know how to build it into their town plan strategy. Any location which shows average rental growth significantly below the national average may be failing to attract occupiers. Equally, any location which is showing abnormally high rental growth may have urban land management problems which should be faced. With so many towns and cities failing to outperform inflation, there are growing signs that institutions would like to invest in sectors other than simply purchase offices, industrial and retail property. A Baring, Houston & Saunders survey in 1996 (Table 7.6) found that a significant minority of direct property investors would consider other sectors.

Investment monies into the property industry

The UK property investment market is characterized, as previously discussed, by a high volume of investment finance, relative to the level of owner occupation, available to investors and developers. Bank lending to property companies is a clear indicator of the sums available to the property industry (Fig. 7.3).

Although net new institutional property investment is at a lower level than in earlier decades (Fig. 7.4), new investment continues. The 1990s have also been characterized by the high level of international property investment into the UK property investment market. A number of international investors in the 1980s saw UK property investment as an asset with capital growth investment potential. In the 1990s in an era of low inflation they see it principally as an

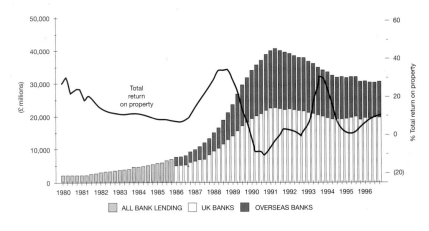

Fig. 7.3. Bank lending to UK property companies has remained over £30 billion in recent years. (Source: Bank of England and Richard Ellis Monthly Index.)

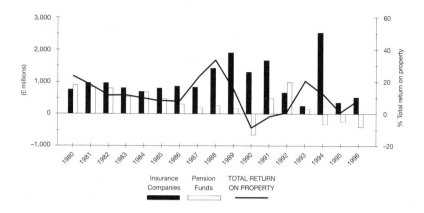

Fig. 7.4. Net institutional investment into property companies from 1980 to 1996 has varied, but generally fallen for Pension Funds. (Source: Office for National Statistics/Richard Ellis Monthly Index.)

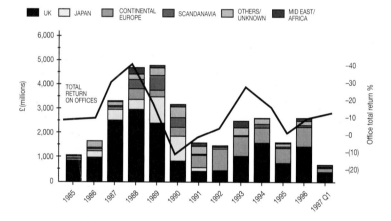

Fig. 7.5. Non-UK investors have become major players in the UK property market. Investment into central London offices since 1985 shows that around 50% of all new investment has come from overseas. (Source: Richard Ellis.)

income-producing asset, and for this reason continental investors are particularly attracted to the central London UK market (Fig. 7.5).

Inflation: the myths and realities

The impact of inflation on the property investment market has historically generated a number of strategies, which have been largely based on a myth. The town planners, property investors, bank lenders and many others have frequently relied on capital growth in the past to achieve financial results. Bank loans have often been short term and have relied upon lenders being able to sell property investments or developments at inflated capital values to enable the bank loan to be repaid. Investors have frequently invested assuming that rental growth over the longer term (together with the downward movement in investment yields) would have the impact of increasing the asset worth of their investments. Town planners have also assumed that developers and investors would be able to make extraordinary capital gains, hence justifying their often arbitrary planning gain requirements.

142

The myth behind all these assumptions has been the concept that property investment is a unique 'hedge against inflation'. This has been extended into even deeper mythology with the concept that 'a little bit of inflation will be good for property investment performance'. History tells otherwise; not only have rental values not always kept pace with inflation, but the total return on property (that is, rental income plus capital growth) has also produced a mixed picture.

Property investment performance and inflation

While capital gains have benefited the astute players in the investment market, it comes as something of a shock to many investors, as well as town planners, to find that year-on-year there is a negative correlation between property investment performance and inflation. As I discussed in an article in 1994, this is clearly illustrated by the fact that, in a number of occasions over the last few decades, rental values (and property investment performance) have moved in the opposite direction to inflation. For instance, property investment perform-ance crashed between 1989 and 1990, yet inflation peaked at over 10% in 1990, at the property investment market's worst hour!

An examination of the year-on-year correlation between inflation and the performance of gilts, equities, direct property and cash since 1962 (the longest dated set of data available) shows that not only is there a negative correlation between inflation and property investment performance, but only yearly returns on cash appear to have a positive correlation. In addition, there has been almost no correlation year-on-year between property investment performance and the performance for gilts and equities. Gilts and equities do, however, correlate with each other.

The analysis presented in Table 7.7 demonstrates that property is not automatically a 'hedge against inflation'; nor is 'a little bit of inflation good for property performance'. An examination of the long-term performance of property, compared with gilts and equities since 1968, shows a slightly different relationship. In the long term, both property and equities have outperformed inflation – property is not unique in having been a long-term hedge against inflation!

As Table 7.8 shows, property has produced an average annual rate of return of 13.3%, higher than the return for gilts at 9.9%, but lower than equities at 15.5%. The average annual real (inflation adjusted) return on property has been 4.6%, compared with only 1.3% for gilts, but 6.3% for equities (Fig. 7.6). Evidence like this clearly disproves Roger Bootle when he says:

	Gilts	Equities	Property	Cash	Inflation
Gilts		0.65	0.07	0.02	0.05
Equities			0.16	–0.09	0.25
Property				–0.26	–0.08
Cash					0.42

NB: The closer the correlation to 1.00, the stronger the relationship between markets.
Source: Richard Ellis.

Table 7.7 Long-term performance year-on-year correlation matrix, 1962–95

Commercial property investments do not seem to have been a very good hedge against inflation: sometimes the reverse.

Year-on-year, as I explained earlier, Roger Bootle's comments apply, but over the long term a different picture emerges. Since 1968 the direct property investment market has only produced a negative nominal return on three occasions, compared with equities which have produced a negative return on six occasions and gilts on seven. The principal difference between the securitized markets (equities and gilts) and direct property is that direct property has produced the lowest standard deviation and the lowest level of volatility: a standard deviation of 11.2% (and a volatility of 0.84%) compared with 17.3% for gilts (with a volatility of 1.75%) and a high of 33.6% for equities (producing a volatility of 2.17%). This is one of the reasons why institutions will remain

Year	Property		Equities		Gilts	
	Nominal	Real*	Nominal	Real*	Nominal	Real*
1968	15.4	10.1	52.1	45.1	−4.9	−9.2
1969	16.7	11.0	−5.2	−9.8	−6.9	−11.5
1970	11.4	4.6	−7.7	−13.4	6.6	0.1
1971	23.1	12.7	39.6	27.9	14.6	5.0
1972	28.7	19.7	15.8	7.7	−6.8	−13.3
1973	27.8	17.1	−28.8	−34.8	−10.7	−18.2
1974	−15.6	−27.2	−51.7	−58.3	−17.9	−29.2
1975	11.0	−10.5	150.9	102.2	41.8	14.3
1976	9.1	−6.4	1.7	−12.8	12.3	−3.7
1977	25.6	8.4	48.6	28.2	50.1	29.5
1978	25.3	15.8	8.2	0.0	−3.3	−10.6
1979	22.0	7.5	11.1	−2.1	4.3	−8.1
1980	23.4	4.6	35.0	14.4	21.1	2.6
1981	18.0	5.5	13.5	1.4	1.4	−9.4
1982	11.5	2.7	28.9	18.7	53.9	41.7
1983	11.2	6.4	28.8	23.2	16.2	11.2
1984	9.5	4.3	31.6	25.3	7.3	2.2
1985	7.8	1.7	20.6	13.7	11.3	5.0
1986	7.9	4.4	27.5	23.3	11.7	8.0
1987	22.4	17.5	8.0	3.7	16.3	11.7
1988	33.9	27.6	11.6	6.4	9.4	4.3
1989	15.4	7.1	36.0	26.2	5.7	−1.9
1990	−8.5	−16.4	−9.7	−17.5	4.2	−4.8
1991	−1.3	−6.8	20.7	14.0	18.6	12.0
1992	1.7	−2.0	20.4	16.0	17.0	12.8
1993	20.8	18.9	28.4	26.4	34.4	32.3
1994	12.8	10.0	−5.8	−8.1	−12.2	−14.3
1995	1.1	−2.3	23.9	19.7	16.4	12.5
Annual average return	13.3	4.6	15.5	6.3	9.9	1.3
Standard deviation	11.2	11.4	33.6	27.6	17.3	15.4
Volatility coefficient[†]	0.84	–	2.17	–	1.75	–

Table 7.8 Annual percentage rates of return: 1968–95

* Inflation adjusted return.
[†] Volaility coefficient is the Standard deviation divided by the Annual average return.
Source: Richard Ellis.

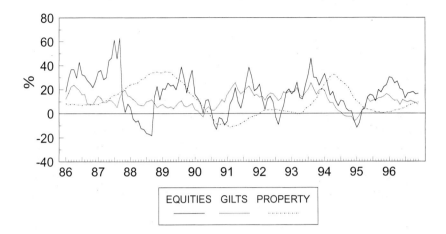

Fig. 7.6. Investment markets' total returns show that, despite the good long-term performance for property, compared with equities and gilts over the last 10 years, the performance has been disappointing. After the booming 1980s, property underperformed for many years. (Source: Financial Times *and Richard Ellis.)*

attracted to property investment and are likely to continue to influence the development of towns and cities.

Investment market yields

In an era of low inflation the outlook for the direct property investment market, as well as for the occupiers of commercial buildings and town planners, is very different from the past. In recent years, compared with the yield on equities and gilts, the initial yield on property investments has been remarkably high. Following the 1980s, when capital values increased and property yields fell to an average of below 6%, the 1990s has seen property investment yields increase (Fig. 7.7). In 1993 the average investment yield was above 10%, and even at the end of 1996 the average initial yield stood at just under 9%, more than half a percent higher than the yield on long-dated government gilts. It should be remembered, however, that the average initial yield in the property market includes both the good and the bad. This yield is very different from the prime yields previously shown on Table 7.2.

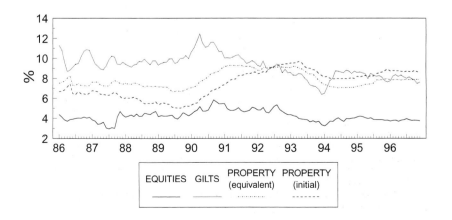

Fig. 7.7. Investment market yields. Compared with the yield on equities and gilts, property now shows a very comfortable initial income yield. (Source: Financial Times *and Richard Ellis.)*

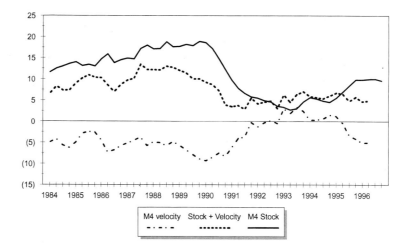

Fig. 7.8. Money Supply (M4) should be related to the velocity of circulation to fully understand the impact of its growth.

The period when property investment yields were abnormally low often reflected a period when capital growth dominated the total performance from property investment. The yield on long-dated government gilts became positive, in real (inflation adjusted) terms, in 1982. The 1980s should have been a period when property investment was dominated by income returns, not capital growth; but in the early 1980s many investors became concerned about building obsolescence, particularly in the office market. However, it was also a period of enormous monetary growth. The money supply grew from around 10% in the early 1980s to around 20% in the late 1980s (Fig. 7.8). The enormous growth of money in the economy (M4 represents all bank and other deposits) had a turbo-charge effect on the property market; and although rental growth was fairly modest in the early 1980s – as one would expect in an era of high real interest rates – by the end of the 1980s strong economic growth and the supply of money in the economy caused occupiers to bid up rental values. Rental growth, year-on-year, increased by more than 20% in 1988, before plummeting by more than 10% in 1990 (Fig. 7.9).

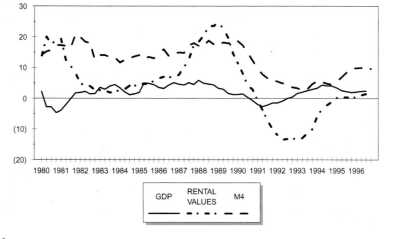

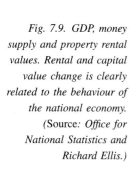

Fig. 7.9. GDP, money supply and property rental values. Rental and capital value change is clearly related to the behaviour of the national economy. (Source: Office for National Statistics and Richard Ellis.)

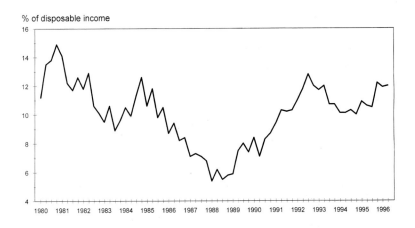

Fig. 7.10. *Personal Saving Ratio 1980–1996; savings are likely to remain under 10% in the future. (Source: Office for National Statistics.)*

In the late 1990s, the money supply had once again started to accelerate. However, by combining the velocity of circulation of money with the growth of the money supply, an implied monetary growth figure showed that a repeat of the 1980s boom was unlikely. The nervousness to spend money and invest was represented by the fact that velocity of circulation was at a relatively low level. This was reflected in the level of savings, and the level of investment in new buildings continuing at a relatively low level (Fig. 7.10).

Future property performance and town and city development

The implications of this major structural change in the financial markets are profound for the property investment markets, and for the future of towns and cities. There were enormous capital gains in some years in the 1970s, during a period of high inflation. The abnormal capital gains in the 1980s were largely attributable to the extraordinary growth in the money supply, rather than to the underlying demand in the economy as a whole. The money supply, and its impact on the property market, contributed towards inflation; it was not that inflation automatically caused capital asset growth.

If we assume that we really are (as Roger Bootle, in his book *The Death of Inflation*, has suggested) in an era of low inflation for the foreseeable future, the high level of income yields now being generated by the property investment market are here to stay. The majority of all property investment performance in the next few years is likely to be generated by income, rather than inflationary gain in capital values (Fig. 7.11). This is a viewpoint I discussed in 1993 in an article entitled 'Valuation methods in the nervous nineties'. The implications for property investors and town planners are important; town and city centres must be efficient to be able to generate high levels of rental income from property investment assets.

Town planning frequently reflects a nostalgia for the past, rather than a coherent strategy for the future. Those strategies which do exist often reflect an objective to maintain what J.K. Galbraith calls 'the culture of contentment' or to prescribe a land use pattern as it ought to be. They should, instead, reflect the changing views of a mature democracy and an understanding of how land use markets have changed and continue to evolve. Town planning must now look

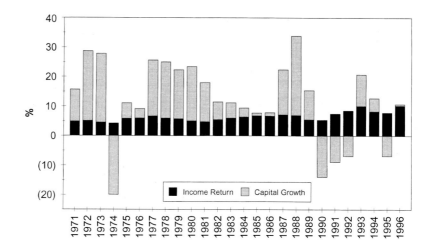

Fig. 7.11. All property total returns. During a number of years in the past, high capital gains were achieved. The outlook shows that the majority of the return from commercial property investment will depend on the rental income, not the capital growth. (Source: Richard Ellis.)

forward. The rental income level of town and cities must be at a sufficiently high level in the future to justify the financing of that property investment; where income levels are low due to poor demand, urban areas will deteriorate. However, in all urban areas town planners will not be able to demand extraordinary planning gains. An era of low inflation raises the spectacle of the forces of urban change differing from recent decades; town planners need to adjust to a new agenda and improve the rental income efficiency of urban locations to be able to compete and survive.

Local authorities and property investment

At the heart of the problem for local authorities is the issue of 'subsidiarity'. This is a concept that has grown out of Great Britain's involvement with the European Union and in theory delegates political power to national or local government as appropriate.

As mentioned in Chapter 1, Charles Handy and others have observed that as monetary policy has been implemented at a national level, taxation powers have been increasingly removed from regional and local governments; the last two decades have witnessed a centralization of political financial power in Great Britain.

In other parts of Europe there are similar conflicts between the wishes of local and national government. In Germany the Lander (the regional governments) have certain powers to raise taxes, as well as to spend money, but even in Germany there is a growing conflict; city powers are limited and there are growing pressures, for instance, for out-of-town property development. In the United States of America there are similar conflicts with city taxes, state taxes and national federal taxes imposed one upon another on a number of goods sold at an individual and corporate level. It is evident, therefore, that unless some means of reconciling these conflicts can be found between the needs of towns and cities versus national objectives, the pressures of market competition are likely to see an on-going process of polarization with some towns and cities being winners, and others being losers.

148

There is no doubt that in Great Britain significant sums are spent both directly and indirectly on urban development. Earlier in this book I refer to Enterprise Zones, Urban Development Corporations, City Grants, Capital Challenge, Assisted Areas and other forms of public finance which have appeared in recent years. Superimposed on all this is the Private Finance Initiative, which was discussed in Chapter 5 concerning the office market and in Chapter 6 in relation to the global economy, and to which I will return later in this chapter.

Financing new town development: a Milton Keynes example

Seeking a formula between public and private finance, with reference to land use developments, is not a new concept. Indeed, it has been around for many centuries. In the early decades after the Second World War significant sums of private finance were invested in the urban fabric of Great Britain. A typical example was the development of Milton Keynes, an area designated as a New City in 1967. By the late 1990s, 30 years later, Milton Keynes had become established with a population in excess of 200 000 persons. In the 1970s a number of institutional investors were encouraged to participate in the birth and growth of this New City. A typical public–private finance arrangement concerned the development of Mount Farm, an employment area (Figs 7.12 and 7.13). The development comprised 28 units in two U-shaped terraces around a central service yard, with units ranging from under 4000 ft^2 to more than 15 000 ft^2. The total development comprised around 170 000 ft^2 on a site area of 8.6 acres.

The financial arrangement that was eventually used between the public and private sectors was as follows: The Milton Keynes Development Corporation agreed to hold the freehold interest of the land but grant the investor a headlease of 125 years at a peppercorn rent, with the investors simultaneously taking back an underlease for the same term on a rent to be agreed, less one

Fig. 7.12. Mount Farm Industrial Investment, Milton Keynes. Funded with a partnership between the public and private sectors using an established leasehold sale and leaseback formula.

Fig. 7.13. Mount Farm Industrial Units, Milton Keynes. An extensive loading area and good road access is necessary for modern industry which cannot be provided in town and city centres.

day. The investor advanced finance in respect of the construction of Mount Farm, including all building fees. Interest was calculated and rolled up at a compound rate of 9% per annum until a maximum capital commitment had been reached. The Development Corporation agreed to provide finance above this maximum commitment. It was agreed that, at a date in the future when the development should have been completed, the Development Corporation would pay the investor a rent under the terms of the lease. The initial rent was calculated at 7% of the investor's total expenditure (provided the expenditure was limited as described above). It was also agreed that the investor's rent would be reviewed every five years, and the rent received would be a proportion of the total rental value of the building calculated at the date of rent review. In summary, the rent was to be based on 7% of the initial expenditure plus half of any rents achieved over and above a target rental level agreed before construction commenced. The Development Corporation undertook to under-let the buildings to occupational tenants at full market rents.

This simple, yet well-tried partnership between the public and private sectors resulted in the investor's income being guaranteed by the Development Corporation, but both parties were able to enjoy the potential increase in rental levels over and above the initial target rent. The agreement further provided for a review of the rent provisions every 30 years.

Considering that such a simple tried and tested formula has been so successful over many decades, and where the transfer of investment risk between the public and private sectors was clearly defined, it is perhaps surprising that the Private Finance Initiative has had such a slow start since it was originally proposed in the early 1990s.

Urban development and the Private Finance Initiative
One of the issues which remains outstanding, and relates to targets met in the Maastricht Treaty, is that of the Public Sector Borrowing Requirement (PSBR). If government raises finance on the gilt market by selling government bonds to private investors, it inevitably creates a PSBR. If, on the other hand, the public sector pursues the Private Finance Initiative route, or reverts to the much simpler freehold/long leasehold formula described above, it is not clear whether the private investment monies form part of the PSBR or not.

The Department of the Environment guide entitled *The Private Finance Initiative and Local Authorities*, released in 1996, suggests that capital investment undertaken by the private sector will not score against public sector capital spending. The document redefines PFI:

> The Private Finance Initiative was launched in 1992 with the aims of improving the quality and quantity of public sector capital projects and of delivering high quality and more cost effective public services. It does this by encouraging partnerships and by involving the private sector more directly in asset provision and operations. The government believes that the PFI should be the route of choice for all public sector procurements when it can deliver superior value for money.

Within this problem remains the issue discussed in an international context earlier. There appears to be confusion in some cases between methods of raising finance (private versus public) and the provision or procurement of public services. The creation of new towns such as Milton Keynes had a very clear public procurement objective. By contrast, the notoriously traumatic national library at St Pancras has had very confused and changing objectives over the years. It is this lack of a clear public procurement goal, rather than the financing methodology, which has resulted in the national library costing more than anticipated and being completed much later than originally envisaged.

The outlook for public–private urban development and local authority budgets

In the Royal Institution of Chartered Surveyors' document *Shaping Britain for the 21st Century*, a commentary of land use and transport, it is suggested that 'local authorities urgently need additional sources of finance'. This is yet another call for local government to be given greater freedom. Clearly there is a need to control inflation, raise taxes at a national level and provide super-regional public services such as defence, a health service and better educational facilities. However, unless some formula can be found to give local government far greater freedom, physical town planning will remain largely impotent. The current wave of affluent residents, astute retailers and productivity-seeking employers keeping their distance from town and city centres will continue. The piecemeal approach, where public funds have been injected apparently at random to urban areas once they have reached crisis point, is unsatisfactory. Unless a more coherent approach to public–private urban finance co-ordination can be found, the outlook for investment in many town and city centres in the next century remain bleak.

Local authority budgets currently fall into two categories; the Revenue Account and the Capital Account. The Revenue Account is designed to meet annual expenditure which, if exceeded, results in central government capping its contribution. The sources of finance to meet the Revenue Account are Council Tax (since 1993), Non-Domestic Rates (since 1990) and government grants.

The Council Tax is levied by local councils on the occupiers of domestic property, although this annual tax may be reduced due to the personal circumstances of occupiers. It is based upon a locally calculated tax on the value of dwellings as at April 1991, and set out in eight value bands. The Non-Domestic Rate is collected by local authorities, based upon the rateable value of property multiplied by a Uniform Business Rate. There are transitional arrange-ments, based on valuations in 1988 and 1993, where current rateable assess-ments are significantly different from values in these years. All sums collected are paid into a national non-domestic rating pool and then redistributed on the basis of the adult population figure as prescribed by the Secretary of State. Central government grants are then paid to support revenue expenditure so that each local authority providing a standard level of service can set a similar Council Tax. The largest item of expenditure is education, with social services, police, transport, environment services and housing also claiming significant sums of money.

Local authorities (including county councils and unitary authorities) have very little freedom to raise extra revenue that is not controlled by central government. Their role is largely that of an administrator of national policy. For instance, Agenda 21 arising out of the Earth Summmit in Rio de Janeiro in 1992, imposes certain environmental obligations on local government aimed at sustainable development principles. Embarking upon 'slum clearance' expenditure, such as the acquisition of land similar to the Comprehensive Development Area programmes which grew out of the Town and Country Planning Act 1962, is nowadays extremely difficult to implement. Even where local authorities sell assets there are 'set aside' restrictions (normally 75% for council housing and 50% for other assets). The net Useable Capital Receipts, as with other capital expenditure, require central government credit approval before being spent.

The recent Private Finance Initiative suggests that this new form of private–public partnership involving capital expenditure will not score against public sector capital spending limits. The Design Build Finance Operate (DBFO) programme aims to give authorities discretion to make their own choices on expenditure priorities. One of the concepts is to transfer risk for the maintenance, renewal and replacement of investments, but also to transfer the facilities and energy management to the private sector. At least 20% of the payment, it is suggested, should be based upon the performance of the private operator. The key to this new public sector agenda suggests 'where the PFI approach to procurement cannot demonstrate value for money, the PFI option should not be implemented'.

The pros and cons of the PFI

There are clearly a number of arguments in favour of this new central government approach to local authorities finance.

- The PFI programme focuses attention on the issue of value for money. The cost of procuring a facility such as a school, library or public convenience is examined in detail, as well as the method of financing. Is it needed? Where should it be located? How should it be designed? What is the trade off between better design/higher cost and lower specification/reduced cost?
- The private sector may have benefits to bring to the investment, of which traditional local government is not aware. However, the private sector may not always have the better solution to a problem.
- The PFI route reduces the stress on the Public Sector Borrowing Requirement at a time when there is pressure for central government to constrain expenditure, partly to contain inflation, but also to meet the Maastricht Treaty criteria.

Against this new programme there are a number of arguments that:

- PFI is an extremely complicated method of attracting private expenditure. Unlike the simple sale, lease and leaseback formula tried successfully in many new towns, PFI creats a problem.
- How does the private sector quantify the transfer of risk to the satisfaction of the public sector?
- Rather than purchasing their own facilities, are local authorities mortgaging their future to private investors?

- It is obvious that the cheapest source of debt finance is obtainable by government selling bonds in the securities market. PFI is always going to be a more expensive source of finance.

- PFI, despite contracts of 20 years plus being discussed, places the emphasis on a relatively short time horizon, as demanded by the private finance market. Expenditure on New Towns and more recently Urban Development Corporations were an act of faith. It may be a full generation before such expenditure matures. For instance, the total cost of the London Docklands, in terms of public expenditure and tax receipts waived, is likely to exceed £1 billion, and some have suggested it may exceed £2 billion. The Year 2010 will be the earliest date to judge the success of this public expenditure; Milton Keynes, for example, has taken 30 years to mature.

- The worst aspect of the current PFI programme is the reactive rather than proactive impact it is having on local government expenditure. The emphasis understandably is on saving costs to provide facilities. If a local authority can acquire land on the edge of a town at agricultural prices, grant itself planning permission, enter into a private joint venture partnership and enjoy the fruits of its endeavours, that will be the preferred route.

- What a local authority is unlikely to do is enter into a loss-making land acquisition in an inner town or inner city location and redevelop knowing that directly or indirectly the town will benefit. Any additional non-domestic rate income generated will disappear into the national non-domestic rating pool – that is, assuming the investment programme is permitted in the first place!

Alternatives to local authority finance

Town and city investment by the public sector is extremely ad-hoc. Firstly, there are funds from the European Union.

- The European Regional Development Fund provides joint venture finance for the provision of infrastructure. Merseyside and the Scottish Highlands and Islands have benefited from this fund.

- The European Social Fund is primarily concerned with training and education.

- The Financial Instrument for Fisheries Guidance and the European Agricultural Guidance and Guarantee Fund assist fisheries and farming with only an indirect impact on urban areas.

- The Cohesion Fund relates to the development of infrastructure targeted to assist states achieve the Maastricht Treaty objectives.

In addition to these funds and other national investment programmes there is such expenditure as national transport investment. There is no doubt that the various Lottery Funds are also likely to have an impact on urban development, including the Millennium Fund. It is estimated that on average every household now spends over £2 per week on the National Lottery. Eventually this source of quasi-taxation will be recirculated.

In recent years the government in the UK has lumped together a number of existing programmes into the Single Regeneration Budget. Table 7.9 presents a

Programme	Amount (£m)
Urban Development Corporations	286
Housing Action Trusts	88
English Partnerships	181
Estate Action	373
City Challenge	213
Urban Programme	83
Task Forces	16
City Action Teams	1
Safer Cities	4
Section II (Part)	60
Ethnic Minority Grant/Business	6
Programme Development Fund	3
TEC Challenge	4
Local Initiative Fund	29
Business Start Up Scheme	70
Education Business Partnerships	2
Compacts	6
Teacher Placement Service	3
Grants for Education Support and Training	5
Regional Enterprise Grants Initiative	9
Total Single Regeneration Budget	1442

Table 7.9 The Single Regeneration Budget 1994–95

Source: Tony Baldry, MP, Parliamentary Written Answer: *Hansard* 31.03.94, Col. 918.

Parlimentary Answer in 1994, illustrating the ad-hoc varieties of finance currently available. What emerges from this review of local authority finance is not only the ad-hoc plethora of money available, but also the constraints on how it is spent. At a town, city or regional level the opportunities to create a coherent business plan to meet both social and financial objectives are extremely limited. Unless physical town planning powers can be combined with a greater understanding of the structural changes taking place in the economy, and unless those powers are linked to legal and financial powers, private investment monies will only return to many town and city centres erratically.

However, it has been suggested that if local government is given the freedom to pursue these objectives, it may also be necessary to reduce the number of local and county councillors, pay councillors a full salary similar to the salaries paid to members of Parliament and considerably reduce, but also enhance in calibre, the number of local authority employees. In an increasingly competitive world it is the quality not the quantity of employment which generates greater productivity.

CHAPTER 8
Strategies for the future

To develop a strategy for the future relating to how town and cities may develop in the twenty-first century, it is necessary to identify the 'certainties' which will influence urban change. By 'certainties' I refer to those changes which have occurred gradually over the years but which are now in existence and are unlikely to be reversed. However, before considering how town and city centre managers and investors in urban property should develop a strategy, in the following paragraphs I have deliberately repeated a number of the issues discussed earlier in the book. These are meant more as an *aide memoire*, rather than as a totally comprehensive list of all the forces for change.

- **Financial deregulation** of the world's economies is here to stay. The pressures on countries to compete will increase as more countries embrace the opportunity of opening their borders and businesses to foreign competition. Towns and cities in all countries, particularly in mature economies like Great Britain, will continue to suffer directly and indirectly as they face the pressures of greater world competition.
- **Corporate change** will continue in both the private and public sectors of the economy. This is largely driven by the necessity to become more efficient. Many countries are now trying to reduce their public sector, while the private sector is tending to use people and building more productively to enhance profitability. Towns and cities which are perceived to be inefficient, particularly in terms of transport infrastructure, will lose employment.
- **Technology**, particularly the growth of electronic information technology coupled with the growth of air and road technology, will have a significant impact on towns and cities. The onward march and the impact of technology is relentless! In previous decades geographers have talked about 'footloose' industries; in the information age a more appropriate phrase

would be 'communication mobile' employment; modern technology enables the jobs to move to the people.

- **The meritocratic élite** will dominate urban development. As the job market shrinks in both the manufacturing and service sectors of the economy, an élite workforce, able to develop or utilize information technology, will dominate the world economy. This meritocratic élite will have specific locational preferences in terms of where it wishes to live and work, but increasingly this hub of employment will be the key to an employment multiplier effect on towns, cities and regions.

- The **polarisation of wealth** may be an inevitable consequence of the move towards an economic régime dominated by market forces rather than government intervention. While the salaries to the meritocratic élite may continue to grow in real terms, salaries at the other end of the polarization scale may change very little in the decades to come. This may have a significant impact on retailing. Since the wealthy tend to save more, as a percentage of income, than poorer families the overall impact may be a switch from consumption to savings.

- **Demographic change** will result in an ageing population; in all mature economies the fastest growing sector of the economy will be those aged over 80 years old. The burden of pension provision, whether borne by the public or the private sector, will be a significant drain on the finances of a country with an ageing population.

- **Urban crime** will continue, and perhaps increase. The causes of crime are complex but the reality is that greater crime creates great inefficiency. Taxes inevitably rise to pay for prisons and police forces. Insurance premiums inevitably increase. Crime deters investment and increases investment risks. Urban crime tends to be higher in those areas where there is a imbalance in terms of the socio-economic residential population. The general increase in inequality already referred to may generate an increasingly violent society.

- **Education**, and the quality of education, will be increasingly important in a competitive world. The meritocratic élite will not be able to compete on a world stage unless they are well educated; for the many, education will be necessary for life enjoyment and spiritual fulfilment. But education will not end abruptly in the first age but will continue to the second age (normal working years) and into the third age (normal retirement years). People will try to top up their skill levels in order to improve their employment prospects or as a leisure activity.

- **Convenience retailing** will continue to gravitate away from town centres. Large food stores trade far more efficiently away from areas of urban congestion; both retailers and the shopping public have a preference for this style of retail facility.

- **Comparison retailing** will also continue to gravitate away from traditional town centres, to those retail locations which are accessible by road and good public transport and are well managed.

- **Leisure time retailing** and social activities will increase as a natural product of growing affluence. Traditional areas of retail expenditure, as well as traditional retail locations, will increasingly compete with leisure time-spending activities, including foreign holidays.

- **Town centres** will continue to decline as the natural location for discretionary retail and leisure expenditure. The future of town and city centres may depend upon the growth of middle-income residential development.
- **Employment** will increasingly reflect where people want to live, not where politicians think people should work. Market forces are far stronger than political wishes. Employment hotspots will occur in those geographic locations where the meritocratic élite wish to reside.
- **Employment growth** will take place in those sectors of the economy which cannot be replicated by information technology. Employment growth sectors already include social work, education and the leisure industry. Business services able to design or use information technology, however, will be the dominant employment growth sector.
- **Urban land management** will be concerned with far more than simply appointing a town centre manager. Politicians, in a democracy increasingly influenced by global market forces, will be faced with the dilemma; long-term urban strategies may not appeal to the limited horizons of the electorate. The pressures to use private finance rather than public expenditure, coupled with the restrictions on raising or providing finance at a local government level, may continue to result in 'short termism'. Urban investment decisions may be made on the basis of a short time span 'pay back' period or a satisfactory internal rate of return over an investment horizon of less than 20 years. A longer term coherent strategy should be developed if possible, as the NIMBY (not in my back yard) mentality will continue to persist.

Town and city centre managers: a strategy for the future

The next few paragraphs set out issues important to local and regional government, but may only be achieved if central government understands the issues concerned.

Residential population

Town and city centre planners should use the demographic computer-based datasets showing socio-economic trends. They need to set clear planning targets to achieve a balanced community. For many towns and cities there is an imbalance with a higher percentage of lower socio-economic groups living in the city centres, and the more affluent living in the suburbs or beyond. A clear target should be set to reverse this trend; creating an urban area to attract middle-income residents, with or without children, able to accommodate car spaces, is vital to the future success of towns and cities. Better educational facilities in city centres are vital but 73% of all households in the upper-income group have two or more cars, compared with only 24% of the national average. Car parking is an inevitable necessity for creating an urban socio-economic residential balance.

Culture

A socio-economic balance will not be achieved unless mixed culture is attracted back into city centres. This ranges from improving the physical environment to the provision of (or encouragement of) such cultural activities as the performing arts, sports and religious activities. Urban managers must set a clear agenda, not just to attract a 'flagship' cultural statement but look at cultural activities at all socio-economic levels and create a mixture of activities. Clear employment targets should be set in the culture/leisure sector; it is one of the growth employment sectors in the national economy. The challenge is surely to attract employment back into town and city centres.

Transport

Improvements to transport are an inevitable necessity to improving the efficiency of all towns and cities. There may be limits to how well the road system can be improved but there ought to be a positive, rather than a negative, approach to car parking. Accessibility within a city centre also means improving pedestrian and cycling routes. The objective should be to reduce the necessity to use cars for short distances within urban areas.

Shared public transport is essential to urban efficiency. In all towns and cities minor improvements to existing systems, such as improvements to the interchange facilities between rail and bus transport, are essential. All towns and cities need a regular (but independent) review of their transport systems. A five-yearly review involving a short report from a transport expert should be a minimum requirement in all towns and cities. Each quinquennial report should be provided by a different transport expert so that fresh ideas are being presented on a regular basis each time a report is produced.

In a world influenced by global economic events, air transport, and access to international roads, rail, air and water transport systems, should also be continually reviewed. Every town and city in Great Britain needs good access to an international point of entry and exit; each town and city is competing in the global economy as well as with other centres within Great Britain.

Retailing

Town and city centres must identify future types of retailing appropriate to their location. To simply assume that the dense retail activity in town centres, which grew enormously between 1945 and 1990, will remain is naive. Town and city managers need, at least every five years, to conduct a survey (perhaps by telephone) of changing retail consumer trends and to manage the downsizing of retail activity; they need to have a proactive approach to alternative uses in town and city centres. Leisure and/or residential uses for redundant retail builds should be actively encouraged, but there must be a far better understand of the physical, managerial and investment risk limitation of 'mix use' development.

Employment

Unless towns and cities understand the traumatic employment changes taking place at the current time at a national and international level, they will not be able to benefit from such change. All towns and cities competing for their survival should periodically undertake market surveys to gain a better under-standing of how the business community perceives their town or city as a business location. Such research should then be used either to market the town (changing misconceptions of a particular urban location) or to develop an employment–land use strategy appropriate to the market's perception of that town or city as a place for job creation. Unless urban managers understand that jobs increasingly follow where people want to live (not the other way round) their strategies will waste money and will be doomed to failure. All urban managers should look at employment growth sectors, rather than 'flog a dead horse' by encouraging employment in sectors which are clearly declining.

Changing investment values

While recognizing the inevitable conflicts between national and local finance, with implications for resource allocation between competing claims and the needs to control inflationary expenditure, all towns and cities should be aware of property investment value changes. Nowadays there is no excuse; there is far more data available on property investment values in Great Britain at a town level than in any other country in the world. This should be used as an urban management tool. All urban managers should assess, even if it is a very general assessment, how the asset base of their urban area is changing. As with a limited company, they should create a balance sheet to review not just how their physical assets are changing in value, but how those changes compare with other towns and cities and the property investment market generally.

Urban property investment: a strategy for the future

The preceding paragraphs were addressed to local and regional government. The following issues relate to urban developers, investors and occupiers in the private sector. The astute reader will notice that the list of issues is identical to the preceding paragraphs, but deliberately in reverse order.

Changing investment values

While acknowledging that all short-term private investment decisions should involve an element of arbitrage (buying at a price below the perceived long-term investment worth), over the medium to long term all investors need to understand how the balance of supply and demand for urban property is likely to change, and hence influence investment decisions.

In recent years an increasing amount of potential interest has been paid to investment trends, although don't forget that 'where there's muck there's brass' may be true. However, many investors now use econometric modelling to predict short-term changes in rental and capital values. As a matter of course, all private investors should undertake an internal rate of return (discounted cash flow) assessment of all existing and potential property investments, and balance this calculation against other assessment methods. There are, however, a number of longer term issues which should also be taken into consideration.

Employment

All investors need to gain a better understanding of employment trends. A simple investment criteria is to price investments according to where the meritocratic élite want to live. This does not mean that investments should be ignored in those areas where residential populations are falling, particularly if new forms of employment, such as in the leisure industry, are expanding. What it does mean is that being aware of employment change provides a strategy for understanding property market prices and future investment worth.

As all investors and developers know, the market price influences development decisions; therefore, the market price must exceed the development cost if construction is to take place. If the market price is too low, or perceived to be falling, investment decisions will be inhibited.

Retailing

The on going decline of retail activity in town and city centres is inevitable. This does not mean that city centres should not be the locations for investment and development activity by the private sector. What it does mean is that all investors must recognize urban change; retailing on the edge of or outside town centres has grown significantly over the last decade and this growth is likely to continue.

Retail investment is increasingly linked to leisure time activities; unless investors understand this long-term trend, they are liable to misunderstand investment performance and investment expectations will not be realized by financial fulfilment.

Transport

All investors need to look carefully at the transport strategies employed by towns and cities. Some cities have a very proactive approach to transport, and there are examples of developments that have a far higher level of car parking than is generally available. These developments have also been very successful. Road access and car parking will continue to dominate urban change, but no property investor should ignore improvements in public transport, including park-and-ride facilities as well as the development of urban light rail–tramway systems.

Culture

Cultural attractions in all towns and cities, including arts, sports and religious activities, are normally not considered as significant by investors. However, in developing a medium- to long-term investment strategy for any urban area, investors should consider the overall cultural infrastructure of a town and city. Is there a proactive approach to the town and city by politicians towards cultural improvement in a particular urban area? The dramatic improvements in the centres of some cities have clearly influenced property investment performance. Urban property investors over the longer term ignore cultural improvements at their peril.

Residential population

The meritocratic élite will dominate the job market in the twenty-first century. Knowledge-based workers, using information technology to their advantage, will attract the higher salaries and have an impact on urban development. Urban property investors not only need to be aware of this change, but should examine how urban managers in a particular geographic area are managing to attract such a workforce in a globally competitive marketplace. The failure of a town to move towards a balanced socio-economic residential population may produce disappointing financial investment results over the longer term.

References

Chapter 1

Barbara Castle, *Fighting all the Way*, Macmillan, 1993

Diane Coyle, Old Master's theory fails to solve New Labour dilemma, *The Independent*, 25 April 1996

Department of the Environment, *Planning Policy Guidance Note 6*, Consultation Paper, July 1995

Jonathan Glancey, Exit from the city of destruction, *The Independent*, 23 May 1996

Charles Handy, *The Empty Raincoat*, Arrow Books, 1995

Will Hutton, *The State We're In*, Vintage, 1996

Jane Jacobs, *The Death and Life of Great American Cities*, Jonathan Cape, 1962

Mike Jenks, Elizabeth Burton and Katie Williams, *The Compact City*, E & FN Spon, 1996

Nigel Lawson, *The View from No.11*, Bantam Press, 1992

Geoffrey Lean, The greedy city, *The Independent*, 14 April 1996

Peter Martin, *Third Millennium Management*, Bathos Press, 1997

Professor Patrick Minford, *Liverpool University Economic Commentaries*, 1993

Geraldine Pettersson, Crime and mixed use development. In *Reclaiming the City*, ed. A. Coupland, E & FN Spon, 1996

J.R.S. Revell, *The Wealth of the Nation*, Cambridge University Press, 1967

Stephen Shaw, A ball market for prisons, *The World in 1997*, The Economist.

Robert Skidelsky, *The World after Communism*, Macmillan, 1995

Alvin Toffler, *Future Shock*, The Bodley Head, 1970

Richard Tomkins, Fix that broken window, *Financial Times*, 27 December 1996

Keith Vaz, *Reinventing The City*, *City 2020*, New Labour, 1996

Keith Vaz, *Planning for Prosperity*, New Labour, 1996

Keith Vaz, Speech on *Planning for Prosperity* at Canary Wharf, 20 September 1996

Chapter 2

Anon., The battle to keep Vancover livable, *Macleans Magazine* (Canada), January 1971

Anon., 'The impossible dream?', *The Economist*, 13 July 1996

Anon., The ultimate high rise, *San Francisco Bay Guardian*, 1971

Anon., Inequality, *The Economist*, 5 November 1994

Bryan Anstey, City of tomorrow – Barbican and beyond, *Journal of the Royal Institution of Chartered Surveyors*, June 1995

Charles Bain, Towns to grow in greenfields, *The Independent*, 1 August 1996

Barbican Press Release, September 1970

T.B. Bottomore *Elites and Society*, C.A. Watts & Co., 1964

M. Breheny and P. Hall *The People – Where Will They Go?*, Town and Country Planning Association, 1996

Andy Coupland (editor), *Reclaiming the City, Mixed Use Development*, E & FN Spon, 1996

Nicholas Crafts and Gianni Toniolo, *Economic Growth in Europe since 1945*, Cambridge University Press/CEPR, 1996

Department of the Environment, *Revised PPG6: Consultation Draft*, July 1996

Disneyland Paris, *The City in 2020*, Publishing Business, 1995

English Partnerships, *Annual Report & Financial Statements*, 31 March 1995

David Eversley, Business news, *The Sunday Times*, 13 June 1971

David Eversley & David Donnison, *London, Urban Patterns, Problems and Policies*, CES, 1973

Cheryl Freadman, Rags to riches, *Estates Gazette*, 3 August 1996

John Kenneth Galbraith, *The Good Society*, Sinclair-Stevenson, 1996

John Gummer, *Housing Growth: Where shall we Live?*, HMSO, November 1996

Peter Hall, David Eversley Obituary – The urban warrior of planning, *The Guardian*, 10 July 1995

Roy Hattersley, Time to knock them down, *Independent on Sunday*, 8 September 1996

Tom Hayes and Jane Flanagan, Has your area gone up or down?, *Evening Standard*, 15 January 1996

Richard J. Herrnstein and Charles Murray, *The Bell Curve*, Free Press Paperbacks, Simon & Schuster, 1996

Judy Hillman, Towering costs, *The Guardian*, 23 November 1971

Judy Hillman *Planning for London*, Penguin Special, 1971

Anthony Jay, *Corporation Man*, Jonathan Cape, 1972

Mike Jenks, Elizabeth Burton and Katie Williams, *The Compact City*, E & FN Spon, 1996

Richard Lawton, The journey to work in Britain, some trends and problems, *Regional Studies*, Volume 2, No. 1.

Norman Macrae, The thieving state, *The World in 1997*, The Economist

Geoff Marsh, *Residential Development in Central and Inner London, 1995*, London Residential Research Limited

Geoff Marsh, *Residential Development in Central and Inner London, 1996*, London Residential Research Limited

Robin Morris, *How to Save the Underclass*, Macmillan, 1996

Angus P.J. McIntosh, A study of a residential area in relation to travel time cost saving, BA Degree dissertation, University College of North Wales, Bangor, 1972

Lewis Mumford *The City in History*, Secker & Warburg, 1961

Alan Rowley, *Mixed-Use Development*, RICS, 1996

Sir Richard Rogers, *Reith Lectures*, BBC, 1995

Frank Schaffer, *The New Towns Story*, Paladin, Granada Publishing, 1972

Stephen Shaw, A bull market for prisons, *The World in 1997*, The Economist

E.F. Schumacher, *Small is Beautiful*, Blond & Briggs Limited, 1973

Mark Suzman and Motoko Rich, Nursing home operators look for healthier future, *Financial Times*, 9 May 1996

J. Tetlow and A. Gross, *Homes, Towns and Traffic*, Faber & Faber, London, 1965

Keith Vaz, *Reinventing The City, City 2020*, New Labour, 1996

Chapter 3

Anon., Technology and unemployment, *The Economist*, 11 February 1995

Asa Briggs, *Victorian Cities*, Odhams Press, 1963

G. Bannock, R.E. Baxter and E. Davis, *The Penguin Dictionary of Economics*, Penguin Books, 1991

R. Beeching, *The Reshaping of British Railways*, HMSO, London, 1963

Colin Buchanan *et al., Traffic in Towns*, HMSO, London, 1963

Bill Gates, *The Road Ahead*, Viking, 1995

Ebenezer Howard, *Garden Cities of Tomorrow*, Attic Books, Powys, Wales, 1898

Angus P.J. McIntosh, Urban land investment in relation to rail transport, MPhil. thesis, University of Reading, 1978

Microsoft®, *Encarta*, 1995

Lewis Mumford, *The City in History*, Secker & Warburg, 1961

Ralph Nader, *Unsafe at any Speed*, USA, 1965

National Travel Survey, Department of Transport, 1996

Jeremy Rifkin, *The End of Work*, G.P. Putnam's Sons, 1995

G.I. Savage, *An Economic History of Transport*, Hutchinson, 1966

Martin Wolf, Trade is not to blame, *Financial Times*, 10 December 1996

Chapter 4

Anon., Focus on retail demand, *Property Intelligence*, 1996

Anon., The cities come back to life, *The Economist*, 6 July 1996

Anon., Reviving cities. Has Cleveland mortgaged its tomorrows?, *The Economist*, 20 July 1996

Colin Buchanan *et al.*, *Traffic in Towns*, HMSO, London, 1963

Nigel Cope, Retailers are trying to hold back the Internet tide, *The Independent*, 23 August 1996

Angus P.J. McIntosh and Jo Bacon, *UK Retail Market Bulletin*, Richard Ellis, 1996

Oliver Marriott, *The Property Boom*, Hamish Hamilton, 1967

Russell Schiller, Town-centre winners and losers, *Estates Gazette*, 14 July 1996

Alan Tate, *Planning and Retailing*, Retail Report, Healey & Baker, 1985

Barry Wood, Some preliminary findings on the spatial consequences of the impact of information technology (IT) on retail activity, *RICS Cutting Edge Conference*, Bristol, 1996

Chapter 5

Anon., *Britain's Best Cities for Business: An Annual Survey 1996*, Black Horsel Relocation

Anon., *The British Office Market: Occupiers' Preferences and Tomorrow's Workplace*, Richard Ellis, 1995

Anon., White-collar factories, *The Economist*, 25 November 1995

Ian Angell, The signs are clear: The future is inequality, *The Independent*, 25 September 1996

Colin Amery, Crazed dream of a phoenix from ashes of a razed library, Norwich, *Financial Times*, 2 April 1996

Leyla Boulton and Gilham Tett, Race on to clear the air, *Financial Times*, 5 August 1996

Disneyland Paris, *The City in 2020*, Publishing Business, 1995

Francis Duffy, *The City Revolution: The Workplace Revolution*, Healey & Baker, 1986

Angus P.J. McIntosh, The property market and the third employment revolution, *Estates Gazette*, 1 July 1995

Angus P.J. McIntosh, *National Office Survey: The Workplace Revolution*, Healey & Baker, 1986

Douglas McWilliams, *London's Contribution to the UK Economy*, London Chamber of Commerce & Industry/CEBR, 1996

Stuart Morley, The future for offices, *Estates Gazette*, 3 August 1996

Jeremy Rifkin, *The End of Work*, G.P. Putnam's Sons, 1995

Richard Wolfe, Birmingham aims for high-tech solution to cash crisis, *Financial Times*, 2 August 1996

Chapter 6

Anon., *Office Markets of the Future*, The L&B Real Estate Report, Spring 1996

Ted Bardacke, Bangkok may ban new cars until 2001, *Financial Times*, 8 July 1996

Roger Bootle, *The Death of Inflation*, Nicholas Brealey, 1996

Stan Bullard, Ohio development markets, *Urban Land Magazine*, April 1996

M. Walter D'Alessio and Gregory R. Brynes, Philadelphia development markets, *Urban Land Magazine*, October 1995

John Kenneth Galbraith, *The Good Society*, Sinclair-Stevenson, 1996

John Kenneth Galbraith, *The Affluent Society*, Hamish Hamilton, 1958

John Kenneth Galbraith, *The World Economy Since the War*, Sinclair Stevenson, 1994

Nigel Lawson, *The View from No.11*, Bantam Press, 1992

Angus P.J. McIntosh, New cities, old favourites, *The World in 1996*, The Economist Publications

Angus P.J. McIntosh, The property market and the third employment revolution, *Estates Gazette*, 1 July 1995

Peter Miscovich, The return of office development, *Urban Land Magazine*, May 1996

Lewis Mumford, *The City in History*, Secker & Warburg, 1961

Michael Prowse, A deep debt of gratitude, *Financial Times*, 25 November 1996

Jeremy Rifkin, *The End of Work*, G.P. Putnam's Sons, 1995

Robert Skidelsky, *The World After Communism*, Macmillian, 1995

Richard Ellis, *World Rental Levels*, Various dates

Chapter 7

Jeremy D.B. Bayliss and Roger Chamberlain, *Shaping Britain for the 21st Century*, RICS, July 1996

Roger Bootle, *The Death of Inflation*, Nicholas Brealey, 1996

Department of the Environment, *The Private Finance Initiative and Local Authorities*, HMSO, 1996

Oliver Marriott, *The Property Boom*, Hamish Hamilton, 1967

Angus P.J. McIntosh, (with S.G. Sykes), *A Guide to Institutional Property Investment*, Macmillan, 1985

Angus P.J. McIntosh, Inflation: the property market myth, *Estates Gazette*, 16 July 1994

Angus P.J. McIntosh, The Efficiency of European Economics and their property markets. *RICS Cutting Edge Conference*, 1994

Angus P.J. McIntosh, Valuation methods in the nervous nineties, *Estates Gazette*, 14 August 1993

Angus P.J. McIntosh, *The 'Real' Case for Property*, Richard Ellis, 1997

John Plender, *That's the Way the Money Goes*, Andrew Deutsch, 1982

B.P. Whitehouse, *Partners in Property*, Birn Shaw, 1964

Index